GIVE
and
TAKE

GIVE
and
TAKE

David Read

CITI OF
BOOKS

CITIOFBOOKS, INC.
3736 Eubank NE Suite A1
Albuquerque, NM 87111-3579
www.citiofbooks.com
Hotline: 1 (877) 389-2759
Fax: 1 (505) 930-7244

Ordering Information:
Quantity sales. Special discounts are available on quantity purchases by corporations, associations, and others. For details, contact the publisher at the address above.

Printed in the United States of America.

ISBN-13:   Softcover   979-8-89391-550-1
             eBook   979-8-89391-551-8
             Hardback   979-8-89391-549-5

Library of Congress Control Number: 2025903495

ACKNOWLEDGEMENTS

I would like to thank my Father, the Most High, for entrusting me with the words he has given me in the writing of this book. In discovering the very fact he loves me and what I am able to receive in this love produces a gratitude that is difficult to express at times. I know that during the process of writing this book I was often faced with the depth of some of the word he gave to me. I also understand that this book barely begins the conversation of give and take and I am astounded at the amount of give and take I have seen in the scriptures that had never before revealed themselves to me.

I would very much also like to thank my very best friend my lovely wife Shellie. She has had to endure many of the moments I struggled to understand what God was doing with me. This book is a direct result of the conversations, disagreements, arguments, discussions, spiritual inputs, forgiveness, and enduring love I have had the pleasure of sharing with the one person in the world God knew would have the strength to grow along with me. His blessing shall always be upon her and our love shall always be established through his love and learning to know him better every day.

.

Special Thanks to Kristen Hamilton for a keen eye and wise input.

TABLE OF CONTENTS

PREFACE

Beautiful, isn't it? This thing called life. We have for thousands of years lived, died, built, tore down, loved, and laughed, cried, and mourned. We have seen empires rise and fall, landscapes change, endured floods, and draughts. We have seen evil go unchecked for a time and peace have its moments. Loves have flourished, and loves have been lost. But we are still here, searching, longing for more while sometimes settling for less yet sometimes having a great gain. But through it all, we are still here.

Life is a give-and-take, always has been, always will be. Some, through life experiences, see taking as their only way of being able to live. Some are willing to give. Some take everything they can while some have given all. Each of us daily gives and daily takes.

If we recognize what we take and what we give, we will better understand why we are the way we are and do what we do. The attitudes we have and thoughts we think concerning the things in our lives are developed by and through our experiences of give-and-take - relationships, business, sports, education, religion, marriage, politics, good things, bad things, the list is endless. All are built on what we give to them and what we take from them.

CHAPTER 1

TAKE SALVATION

And this is life eternal, that they might know thee the only true God, and Jesus Christ, whom thou hast sent.

-John 17:3

We must first start with salvation. For many, this may come in varying forms. Some may believe an event turned their life around. Others give credit to a person for changing their life. But this salvation I speak of is more than just turning your life around. It is eternal, the rebirth of your spirit. The journey your soul takes from self-awareness to one of complete dependence upon the One God that gave a sacrifice *for* you. No other god has made a sacrifice for you. All other god's and religions require you to sacrifice to change your inner being. There is one true God – Creator of heaven and earth – who sent His Son, Jesus, to sacrifice for you. This salvation through the name of Jesus ("For there is none other name under heaven given among men, whereby we must be saved." Acts 4:12"), must be taken. No one else, no event, no success, no personal sacrifice will save you - body, soul, and spirit. No one, no single event can give you salvation. We must take it. It is a free gift given by God, by grace, to all, but we must take it. See, give, and take. God is the only one able to give salvation, and we, in order

1

to gain eternal life spiritually, must take it. In order to grow in your spirit, soul, and body you must be born from above by God, through Jesus, with your heart open to the Holy Ghost. Our natural man - the self-awareness, the one that commits sins in our lives, that part of all mankind that has separated us from knowing and understanding God - is not able to gain the dependence upon a Sovereign Being. It is our "self" that commits evil against God.

Today and throughout history each society, culture, or empire has interpreted acts of evil differently. What you may see as evil someone from another time may have seen it as common place. What we need to do is understand the true meaning of evil. What really constitutes evil? When we see what evil is we will better understand our choice in salvation – what God gives us and what we need to take, why we need to take it, and what the consequences are if we choose not to.

In Genesis chapter 2 verses 7-9 God formed man (Adam) out of the dust of the earth, He breathed into man's nostrils the breath of life. Man became a living soul. God then plants a garden in the East in the land of Eden, and this is where He puts the man He has created. Look at this: God planted a garden. He created the earth, animals, plants, fish, and then plants a garden. Very cool, very cool indeed.

For those of you who are scientist and judge everything through the eyes of science as best as science is able to explain try examining creation through the eyes of probabilities. If there truly is a Creator God then He surely employed science in the process. He set physics in place to establish the boundary of the sea (Proverbs 8:29; Job 38:8-10). He used mathematics to measure the foundations of the earth (Job 38:4-5). If the world was created, then the probabilities of God using science are emphatic, because the world in its entirety functions completely within the context of science. What about the unseen things that science is unable to explain? Romans 12:3 tells us God has allotted to each of us a measure of faith. How do you measure faith? Everyone at one time or another has said, "Oh, I have faith it will work," or something similar, so we are familiar with the terminology. We measure the speed of light from across the universe, yet how do we measure faith? All of the people around the world get up every day, breathing, existing surrounded by atoms and electrons and not even taking these things into account, but they exist even though the eye cannot see them in their individuality. Faith is not a tangible that the naked eye is able to gaze upon, just like an atom, yet we see the evidence of the atom just by looking at our own hands and fingers, or anything that we are able to see or breath. So too is faith as it is not something to visually see, but the evidence is all around us. Faith is the evidence of things not seen (Hebrews 11:1). The proof of this are the things that are accomplished by faith, the actions taken by and through the spirit. To measure faith, you must see it in the eyes of the spirit. The Spirit becomes the only instrument with which your measuring should be performed. Everything that we measure has a tool or instrument we use to determine quantity, length, volume, speed, etc. The eyes of the spirit are how we measure faith. If you are reasoning faith without the proper tool to measure with, then the outcome may look confusing to you. Knowing him as Creator by using his faith will open up to you a world of knowledge that you have yet to discover. Looking at evil then must start at creation and be measured by the lack of the faith of God people have taken and became involved in. This creation of God's has been accomplished through his spoken word, which is performed through his faith.

Why a garden and what was the need for a man? In Genesis 2:5, everything was ready to go it just needed water and someone to care for it, "… and there wasn't a man to till the ground.". The Hebrew word for "till" is *abad*, according to Strong's (Strong's 5647 O.T. HGKSB NASB), which is a very detailed word meaning "to work, to toil, to be worked, till, plow, to cause to work, to make weary, fatigued, to serve, to work as a slave." It goes on, but we see this picture beginning to develop that this garden was going to take some hard work to keep it looking like a garden. The garden we will discover was God's plan to execute life with judgement upon sin, upon Satan, and upon disobedience apart from walking with a Holy God.

God needed a being capable of thinking, solving, sweating, working, and maintaining this lovely garden by putting forth effort. Now if that were all there was to it, if that were all He intended for man, than, really, that would have been the end of it. Man would have just worked the garden. But God wanted this relationship, and he wanted His creation to experience relationships, which would develop into fellowship. God saw in Genesis 2:18 it was not good for man to be alone. Adam had all the animals and fowls, which he had named to hang out with, but God knew Adam would need more. God knew Adam needed a helper, one that was suitable for him, so he created from Adam's rib another being that would share the physical tasks, have a different perspective to tending, bringing emotions with a powerful physical relationship to the garden. Working together, incorporating each other's mentalities, attitudes, workmanship, design, perspective, and cooperation to prove the benefits of relationship working together in the unity of love.

However, before the woman was created, God set the man in the garden and gave him instructions. First in Genesis 2:15, man is to "… dress it and keep it.". Second, in verse 16, he is able to eat the benefits of its fruit by taking what the garden produced through his hard work. Thirdly, in verse 17, he is to follow one rule, just don't do this one thing – "thou shalt not eat of it:" (the tree of the knowledge of good and evil). God gave man work instructions, sustenance and a parameter or condition for safe living.

Now the man and woman were doing their thing, working the garden, both unaware of the experience of the failure of sin both naked before each other and before God, and they were not ashamed. No guilt, no failure, no offenses, never having fallen short of an accomplishment. The word "ashamed" giving the meaning of "confusion, embarrassment or dismay when things do not turn out as expected." (The HGKSB NASB Strong's 954). They had never experienced disappointment because things were not going as expected. They were doing what they were created to do and knew of no other way. Until one day, a certain creature, which just so happened to be more subtle, or crafty, sly, and more cunning than the other creatures came to the woman and questioned what she knew.

Adam had already been placed in the garden by God and, as previously stated, had been given instruction. So Adam got to work. God started lining up the animals and birds to have Adam name them all. Adam is working with the animals and cultivating the garden - a lot of hard work. God saw that Adam could use a helping hand, someone to aid him in all this work. Someone to experience this marvelous garden and share it with in a relationship. When Eve came along, it was Adam's responsibility to pass along the instructions given to him by God.

What did he communicate to her? We can't say specifically, but we know what her response was to the serpent that had questioned her. Genesis 3:2, "And the woman said … 'But from the fruit of the tree in the middle of the garden', God has said, 'You shall not eat from it or touch it, lest you die.'" God's original instruction did not include, "do not touch." Man was to tend the garden which meant he was required to touch the plants in order to maintain the garden.

Picture this, if you will. Adam wakes from his deep sleep, and along with the woman, goes through the garden showing the woman the plants, trees, animals, birds, and fish. Adam may have been saying, "Look, Eve, that animal over there I called a bear and that tree there I called a Sycamore". Eve might have asked, "What did you name that creature?" and Adam would have responded, "Oh, that is a lion, isn't that a good name for such a magnificent beast as this?"

Do you get the picture? From our earliest years we are taught the creation of the world and of man then jump right to the fall of man without ever realizing the relationship from God to man to woman. This may not have been an accurate unfolding of the time spent together before the serpent was written into the scene, but it does shed light on the fact they both existed together, working with each other and she was learning from Adam the instructions given from God.

Adam and Eve reach the midst of the garden and come upon the Tree of the Knowledge of Good and Evil. Here is where Adam discusses the instruction God gave him about this particular tree. Now we cannot sit here and tell you that Adam told Eve not to eat of the fruit of this tree and then added, "do not touch" to those instructions, or that Eve had made a decision to insert this into the instructions thinking she needed to emphasize the importance of these instructions. If we, however, look at how men and women interact today with each other we just might obtain a perspective into this conversation. Remember, Eve was a suitable, or capable person, whose responsibilities included aiding Adam in his responsibilities. Men and women often respond to each other with varying perspectives and mindsets often with a difference toward each other. Her knowledge was contingent upon Adam's ability to communicate instruction and it is very obvious she was able to use her own cognitive reasonings. She was from a man, she was a part of him, and she was with him. Either way whether Adam or Eve added the emphasis "do not touch" God's instructions were modified by the man and/or the woman.

Failure to Follow God's Command

In 1 Kings 13 we read the story of a man of God who was starting in verse one "brought by the word of the Lord unto Jeroboam," who was the King of Israel, speaking a prophesy against the altar the King was sacrificing upon. You can read the story for yourself but the point to be made here is not what the man of God spoke against the altar but about the instructions given by God to the man of God. In verse 9 we see God, "commanded", the man (which is the same word used in God's communication to Adam in the garden concerning the tree of the knowledge of good and evil), "You shall eat no bread, nor drink water, nor return by the way which you came." (1 Kings 13:9). Why not eat? Why not drink? Why not go back the way you came? Jesus is the bread of life (John 6:35), the Holy Spirit is the living water (John 7:39), do not go back from where you came (Numbers 14:3-4); you do not change the word of God, you do not quench the Holy Spirit and you do not go back to life in the flesh for this would be showing disregard for your deliverance from bondage. Stay in the Word, live in the Spirit, walk in faith (Ephesians 2:1-5). Following what God speaks by obedience brings life. Disobedience will lead to death. To make a long story short, the man was found sitting under an oak tree, was lied to by another old prophet, and ended up dying from an attack by a lion (Satan roams about like a roaring lion seeking whom he may devour 1 Peter 5:8).

Wow, you might think this seems a bit harsh doesn't it? When God gives a command, it is entirely up to man to obey it or not. To obey brings God's everything to the table - fulfillment of His Word, blessing, peace, justice, protection, love, provision, prosperity, etc.

To disobey simply does not bode well for anyone. We miss out on fulfillment, peace, love, justice, protection, provision, prosperity, etc. In many cases it will bring death. In the case of the man of God not going straight home by another way, not eating nor drinking, cost him his life. He should have never stopped under the oak tree. He should have kept on going to perform the word God spoke to him. When God tells you to do something get after it and do it. Endure through it and get it accomplished. Don't stop, do it. Don't listen to others, even if it sounds good, endure through it. Nehemiah could have listened to others and he would have failed. He knew what God wanted him to do and he endured through it. Jonah balked at being obedient. He didn't get after it which cost him a three-night stay in the belly of a big fish.

Adam knew what God commanded, but his lack of action, his disobedience to the command of God, with what Eve was offering him, even though it sounded good, obviously demonstrated his lack of resolve and the quality of instruction he passed on to Eve. Adam did not do it, he did not endure through it, and it ended in death. Death to what he was created to do - work in the garden. Death in his relationship and walk with a Holy God by being cast out of the garden. Death in his relationship with Eve, she would now have pain in childbearing and her, "… desire shall be for your husband, And he shall rule over you." (Genesis 3:16). Instead of being a helpmeet, someone to aid in tending the garden, they now had positions to fulfill towards each other.[1]

So, here we have it, God gives us instruction, God gives us sustenance, and God gives us commandments. We take those instructions, commands, and sustenance choosing to follow them or

---

[1] Everything is known of God -the creation, the fall of man, the redemption of man, the new life. God is three in one - God the Father, God the Son, and God the Holy Spirit. Man is three in one, Body, Soul and Spirit. The separation in relationship caused by the fall between man and woman is really God knowing what was happening and what was to come. In this particular case, man was placed above the woman because she came from man. The man is to love his wife like Christ loved the Church, thus, becoming a representation of God to man. Man came from God, so God is above man. The woman is the representation of man coming from God. Her desire is to be to her husband this is the same as us. Our desire is to be to God. This is simply a representation. As God gave life to man through creation so woman gives life through conception. Man has taken what God gave as an example in spirit and veiled it in the flesh to confound the truth. We, in our different cultures, religions and societies, through our flesh sin nature, place the woman under man. This is not to be. We were created to become one through intimate relationship just as we are to be one in Christ. There is nothing revealed that does not reveal the triune God. This includes man and woman. We are a shadow, a reflection of God. Therefore, let us not look at our relationships through the veil of sin and flesh but through the perfect light of love. We are to be a help meet for God to share in His work and live in His love, (i.e. the Garden).

not, to do them or not, choosing to use them or not to. Obedience takes us on the path of good while dis-obedience takes us down the path of evil.

All of the previous pages now tie together and brings us to determining what is evil. Is it not all that separates us from a Holy God? Anything that will prevent us from holy dependence upon His instructions, commands, and sustenance becomes evil.

By partaking of the tree of the knowledge of good and evil, we now have the ability to know what is good and what is evil. Evil may be present but will accomplish nothing until action is *taken* to perform it. When this action is taken, we now commit sin. How did this evil come? Through deceit. Eve was deceived, took action based upon this deception and committed sin. Adam took action but not through deception. Adam's sin was a willful disobedience. He knew what God commanded and yet disobeyed it.

Evil's strength, then, is deception. The farther we move away from God the easier and more deceived we allow ourselves to be. The Bible tells us in I Timothy 6:10 the, "… love of money is the root of all evil." Loving something to a point of dependence on it is replacing the one true God, involving all that he is and has for us, with something he has created that we are to have dominion over. Why worship the created and what this world gives us when you can come to know the Creator and all His promises and loving kindnesses?

If evil's strength is deception, then the flip side is disobedience which is the consummation of sin. Willfully not doing what is known to be right now becomes sin, which is a fulfillment of evil, a turning from a dependence upon God. This is truly the center of self. When we live continuously serving our self, we become so accustomed to living in our emotions, making decisions without ever so much as a thought of our Creator that we develop a hardened heart. When you get a world full of people living like this, evil is free to do as it pleases. Now we have become so deceived, so unwilling to be dependent upon God, that we search for anything to fill a void we may not even recognize nor are aware of. We turn to other gods or religion, we turn to improving our inner self, to knowledge or science, politics, or a cause, to an undisciplined life maybe even drugs. We turn to an endless list of ways that all in themselves fall short. We do it because it is what we can understand or grasp or wrap our mind around.

Now enters faith. In Hebrews 3:12 we are instructed to, "take care", that we do not have, "…an evil heart of unbelief." There is action that must be applied in dealing with evil. We are to watch our words, our thoughts, and our actions; we must take care of faith.

Abraham is known as the Father of faith yet in Hebrews chapter 11 we see Abel, Enoch and Noah listed before Abraham because of their actions taken in performing faith. Faith has been from the beginning, it came before us, it is part of God's design.

Abraham took it to a level that would allow the rest of the world to see what real action must be taken in learning true dependence upon our God. All of those listed in Hebrews Chapter 11 took action in a myriad of ways because they believed in dependence upon God. All of these faced evil and overcame, endured, or even suffered some to the point of death, but they still understood there is nothing here that is permanent. This life we live here is not our own, it is not home.

Believing gives hope. Believing gives strength and confidence. Believing takes love and allows it to work. Believing changes circumstances because it is no longer about us, -self- but about knowing God by being dependent upon Him. "Faith is the substance of things hoped for, the evidence of things not seen." (Hebrews 11:1).

So by faith, we are propelled into doing good. Learning to know God by faith produces in us the desire to please God. Doing good, therefore, overcomes evil. Psalm 34:14, Psalm 37:27, and Isaiah 1:16-17 tell us to "Depart from evil and do good."; "Cease from evil, learn to do good." It is funny how we all have the knowledge of good and evil, yet it seems as though evil comes so easily to us, but we have to learn to do good.[2] This is why our parents discipline us. This is why we have rules to keep us from doing wrong.

There are many who do not believe in God yet admit there is evil in the world. The next time you come across someone who professes the existence of God is a myth or stems from pagan worship or even simply man's imagination ask them, "Do you know Him? Have you asked Him to forgive you and come into your heart? Do you know Him? Do you seek Him as your Creator? Do you personally know Him? "Have you prayed to God for something possibly when you were a child and didn't get an answer or your problem wasn't resolved? Have you determined He doesn't exist because of these experiences? He is and was and is to come… do you know Him?

Romans 3:3, "What then? If some did not believe, their unbelief will not nullify the faithfulness of God." (NASB). Evil is absolute proof that God is. If He is truly the God the Scriptures profess him to be than he must be God of all. He knows both good and evil but chooses only good (Acts 14:17 and Isaiah 7:14-16). This is what makes His love so beautiful. This is why love works through good. Doing good, learning to do good, always brings with it some amount of love. Even small acts

---

[2] 3 John 11; "He that does good is of God: he that does evil has not seen God." The scriptures tell us no man has seen God so what is this telling us? Doing good is what God is – Good. You see the elements of God when you see good. The man who does evil is separated from God, he has no dependence upon God, therefore, he cannot see God because God is good. We have not seen God face to face, but we are able to see God in all His works, His tender loving kindness, His mercy, and grace, in His creation, His salvation, His love and the depths of His word. God is love and God is good.

of doing good are an expression of love because God is good, and God is love.[3]

This is where salvation comes in. John 3:3 Tells us we must be born again, or a better rendering would be born form above. The man Jesus is talking with here is a religious leader named Nicodemus who doesn't understand what it means to be born again. He is looking at things through the eyes of the flesh. Jesus on the other hand explains it as flesh and Spirit. John 3:6 Jesus says, "that which is born of the flesh is flesh and that which is born of the Spirit is spirit." We are not being reborn in the flesh we are being reborn in the spirit. God is Spirit, our flesh was separated from him the moment we knew good and evil (Genesis 3:17-19; John 4:24). We are being reborn in the spirit. That which is born of the Spirit – God's Spirit – is a rebirth of our spirit. It is new life by the Spirit of Life.

In all walks of life, in all aspects of knowledge, we cannot have the capacities to know God intimately through our flesh. We must be born from above. If you are trying to formulate a comprehension of who God is through knowledge of the flesh or reasonings or ill experiences all based upon this natural body, you will only come up short. *But*, if you, through the Spirit of God, seek him, confessing Jesus as Lord and ask him to forgive you, you will enter into a new life. This new life will bring forgiveness, healing of broken hearts, mercy, peace, and the love of God so deep you will take a lifetime discovering it's depths.

Let's bring all of this together for our understanding, from Adam not obeying God; to Eve being deceived; to a prophet not enduring what God instructed him to do; to Abraham's acts of faith; to our poor misconceptions of God and the experiences of our lives that form those

---

[3] The battle of unbelief is demonstrated in Abraham and Sarah receiving the child of promise. (Romans 4:18-21). Abraham contemplated or thought about the age of his own body and Sarah's inability to bare children but instead of going by what was in the natural, which would have made him weak in faith, he did not waver in unbelief, in hope against hope he chose good. Knowing that God is the one who gives life to the dead and calls into being that which does not exist. We are dead to sin but alive to God in Christ Jesus (Romans 6:10). Unbelief is one simple decision away from belief.

misconceptions; and to knowing good and evil while discovering the salvation that delivers us all: the common thread is simply this: *freedom*. That's right, freedom. We are free to *take* the salvation Jesus so freely gives us. We are free to choose. Adam had a choice, the man of God had a choice, Abraham had a choice and we have a choice. Free to choose. We may study these examples and see the consequences of the freedoms these people took. For Adam it caused the fall of all mankind. For the prophet it cost him his life. For Abraham, the choice brought faith for us all and that faith bridges the gap from the natural to the spiritual.

All this might best be explained in the Book of John chapter 12. Jesus was at Bethany with Lazarus (the same man Jesus had raised from the dead), being served by Lazarus's sister Martha when her sister Mary took a pound of very costly perfume and began to anoint the feet of Jesus. Now there are two choices made here: one by Mary and one by Judas Iscariot.

Mary anointed Jesus with the expensive oil and her tears. Judas complained that the expensive oil could be sold, and the money used to help the poor. Both of these, at first glance, seem admirable but as we read on John gives us the explanation describing the difference. What Mary chose was a good towards Jesus. What Judas chose, and John doesn't mince words about this, were the actions of a thief because he was in charge of the money bag and had been taking money for himself.

Mary's choice was for good and Judas' choice was for evil. Both had knowledge of good and evil and both chose according to what was in their heart. What was in Mary's heart was a love for the one who had forgiven her (Luke 7:47). What was in Judas' heart was seeking satisfaction for himself. One acted selflessly, the other acted selfishly.

So, here we are, full circle, give and take. What God gives us freely by faith through grace we must willfully receive. If you were given a gift by a friend and they sat it on the table, but you didn't take it than it would benefit you nothing. Give God a chance and take Him at His word, take the benefits of life through salvation. Simply ask Him to forgive you and welcome Him into your heart for cleansing, healing, and life.

If you asked Jesus to forgive you of your sins and accept Him as your Lord and Savior as you read on in this book you shall see these things in a whole new light. Spiritual comparisons may be made with spiritual eyes.

If you have not asked Jesus to forgive you than the judgements and opinions that you formulate will be in the natural mind and you will lack discernment of the spiritual truths God wants to reveal to you. However, when spiritual truths of God's word are applied, whether in the natural or in the spiritual, they will always bring life.

CHAPTER 2

GIVE RESPECT

Wherefore God also hath highly exalted him,
and given him a name which is above every name.

- Philippians 2:9

Each and every one of us have a desire for respect. Whether you come from a broken home, middle class, rich, poor, abused or pampered we all desire some element of respect. Maybe it is a respect for what we have accomplished or simply for an acceptance of who we are.

Respect may show itself in many ways like holding a door open for an elderly person, picking up a dollar someone dropped out of their pocket and giving it back to them, giving a pat on the back to a co-worker. Respect is given every day in so many ways most of which we may not even recognize. The respect the Father gave Jesus in the opening verse above is directly related to the previous verses which speak of being a servant, humbling oneself, and being obedient which result in true respect being given (Philippians 2:7,8). But what is respect? Where does respect find its roots?

The first example of respect shown to us in the Bible is in Genesis chapter 4, Adam and Eve's number one and number two sons, Cain and

Abel are coming to the Lord to bring an offering. Both young men have grown to an age where they have picked up a path doing what each is good at. Cain is a tiller of the ground and Abel a keeper of the sheep. In the course of time each brother brought an offering to the Lord that came from what they did best. Cain of the fruit of the ground, Abel of the firstlings of the flock and their fat portions. Now we read that the Lord had regard or respect to Abel and his offering but not to Cain's.

Why would our Creator see things this way? First, He is omniscient, He knows all, Past, Present and Future. He knows what is in everyone's heart and mind. Second, the preceding events in the garden established man's knowing of good and evil, the ground was cursed for man's sake, but the blood was the life force of all living creatures (Deuteronomy 12:23).

Cain's offering was born from the curse. Man was to labor by the sweat of his brow as the earth would no longer yield its fruit as it once did under God's essence, his glory, and his presence. Remember man was formed from the earth and, by death through his disobedience, he shall return to the earth from which he was formed. This creation we live in demonstrates God in everything, from the rocks that would cry out for Jesus upon His entry into Jerusalem (Luke 19:40), to the trees we see that have bark, sap, and wood fiber on the inside. Three distinct elements yet still one tree, just as the three in one – Father, Son, and Holy Ghost - are.

Man's self- awareness came with the fall of man and the beginning of the curse. Abel, however, is considered righteous and a prophet, so what is the difference between the two brothers and what they offered (1 John 3:12; Luke 11:50-51)? Abel's sacrifice required the shedding of blood, while Cain's sacrifice came from the cursed ground. Abel's sacrifice spoke of the sacrifice and shedding of blood by Jesus Christ to redeem mankind from the curse. Cain was concerned about his "self," not about what was pleasing to God. When Cain became angry that God did not respect his offering he was faced with a decision, repent, and get into God's will or feel sorry for himself and become angry trying to protect his "self". His choice represented the knowledge of good and evil. Adam's first disobedience toward God produced the same choice, repent, or protect his "self". He chose the latter when he spoke, "the woman, which thou gave me." (Genesis 3:12). He pointed the blame to someone else. Eve was not responsible for Adam's decision; Adam was responsible for what he chose.

God's respect towards both boys offering was directed in Spirit, not flesh, always pointing man towards the way to turn from flesh to spirit, from the curse to new life, from protecting self to obeying God. Cain's anger for not receiving respect for what he offered was a direct result of dwelling on self, (self-pity). In chapter 4:8 Cain talked with Abel about it by rehearsing the lack of respect God showed to Cain's offering. How much time had elapsed between the giving of the offering and the encounter in the field we do not know but it is obvious it was something Cain had been thinking on. Family often has different paths each member follows as is true here with Cain a tiller of the ground and Abel being a keeper of the sheep. Sometimes when you work hard to till the ground, plant it, and cultivate it and the livestock comes along possibly eating your crop it may certainly cause malcontent between the two parties. The point here is there was enough conflict going on that Cain's anger reached a level that brought an eruption. Cain was not the master over his emotions and thoughts, which allowed sin, was crouching at the door, to have its desire over him. Cain allowed jealousy and the feeling of being disrespected to consume him to a volatile point. Look at your own reactions when you feel or believe you are being disrespected. How do you respond? Angrily? Do you try to justify yourself to make you feel better? Do you fall into self-pity? Do you shrink away?

Repentance through humility would have led Cain on a far better path. God said in Genesis 4:7 (NASB), "If you do well, will not your countenance be lifted up?" Doing well in this case is to seek God for His love and mercy. Cain's response could just as easily have been, "Forgive me, Lord, I have sinned against you, please direct me in your path and your will." This kind of response turns your eyes from "self" to the Divine, to obedience and knowing all things are from our Creator.

The Root of True Respect

So, what is respect? For us respect is the acknowledgement of that person's right, skill, position, or authority. Abel's position and authority rested in God's will and plan for mankind. Respect does not include ideals. You may respect the right someone has to express their ideals, but, you do not have to respect their ideals. God respected Abel's offering but not Cain's ideals concerning his own offering. It looked good and sounded good to Cain, this is what he labored for, *Surely I may offer this to God*, he may have thought. Ideals, not founded in God's will, do not have to be respected.

Respect is an extension of love, it is kind, it is not jealous, love does not brag and is not arrogant, it does not seek its own. True respect is the same, it is not jealous, does not brag or become arrogant and it does not seek its own. Jealousy, self-promotion, and arrogance (which is the elevation of self over others) will prevent love. Respect based on these attitudes of self is not respect at all, instead it is pride and pride is a self-destructor of humility. Cain's jealousy and arrogance drove him to murder his own brother, he did not act in love, therefore he was unable to respect the truth of Abel's offering. Respect stems from or finds its existence in love. A humble heart will allow love to flow. Arrogance is a blockade to love and a humble heart (James 4:5-6; 1 Peter 5: 5-6).

Most of us have been taught that respect must be earned. It is not. Respect is not earned, it is given. It is not like an award that you can work for or take because you earned it or achieved it. We may only give respect. You cannot take it from someone because you think you deserve it. Anyone who has accomplished a great achievement can tell you that while many may respect the achievement there are still those who just plain won't hand over respect for what was accomplished.

What about those who have been successful in different jobs or sports or artistry yet when they come across someone who is unaware of those successes receive no respect? We may often fool ourselves into thinking we deserve respect when in the face of all mankind there are those who throughout history have done extraordinarily humble, selfless acts, who are the ones truly deserving of respect.

Many will confuse admiration for respect. We become impressed with a feat or accomplishment someone has achieved and we say we respect that person when it is merely admiration. The difference is admiration usually affects our flesh, our self. An example might be an athlete who excels at a particular sport and a young person may see this achievement determining they want to be like the famous athlete. We are making decisions that are influenced by our "self". Respect does not promote itself because its root is in love. When we are able to applaud a person, not for what they accomplish, but for who they are and do so without concern for how we measure up then we are being true in our respect.

The book of Philippians teaches us in chapter 2 that we "… be likeminded, having the same love, being of one accord, of one mind." That we should not be in strife or do things selfishly but that we have the "…same mind that was also in Christ Jesus…" (Philippians 2:2,5). This mind Christ had was one of humility, He came with all the authority of heaven, with the position of being the Word in the flesh, the right of being the Son of God and the skill of faith full of the Holy Spirit. Yet he had the mind of serving and being obedient through humility. This is what should draw our respect. This is what we should follow, not someone who has performed something to a high level, for far too often those same people are capable of letting us down or placing themselves above us. In doing so their true character is exposed and that is the promotion of "self" demonstrating weakness of character. Respect is often drawn, not by what we obtain, but by what we give up.

It is not wrong to admire others but do not let it promote your flesh, rather to seek God's will in what you do and his grace to enable you to do it. Give respect where respect is due with the right intentions, with the right heart, not to elevate yourself. Never think you can force respect from anyone. Not only would you be promoting self, but you now incorporate fear, control, intimidation, oppression, and grief. All of this stems from the knowledge of good and evil, which was brought on by the Father of Lies, Satan himself. True respect may only be given it cannot be taken from anyone.

When you give respect do so with the intent of recognizing the right character that truly does not promote itself over others. Many who have accomplished feats which others have not will show their character by acts: whether of humbleness or of self-promoting acts. If you take the respect that someone is giving and act humbly then you will include all of those who were a part of how you got to where you are. Great accomplishments are never done alone. Someone else was there with an encouragement, with a challenge or with a discipline that helped you strengthen your disciplines, lifted you mentally and spiritually or supported you in confidence of what you are capable of doing. Never take respect for your own personal gain but be willing to give it right back to those who offer it to you. Leadership will spring from these actions and responses.

Looking back on Cain we see how he responded to God in Genesis 4:9. God asked Cain, "Where is your brother?" And he said," I do not know, am I my brother's keeper." His first response to the Holy God our Creator was a lie and a lack of obedience to love one another. He did know exactly where his brother's body lay, and, yes he is his brother's keeper. We are all responsible for the well-being of each other and we do so by showing respect toward one another in a love that is far and away bigger than us.

Once again, give respect where respect is due and take the respect given with humbleness of mind by giving it right back. Let God do the exalting and you will find yourself being less concerned about disrespect and doing that which is pleasing to God. (1 Peter 5:5; Psalm 138:6; James 4:6).

CHAPTER 3

TAKING OFFENSE AND GIVING FORGIVENESS

The best way for us to interpret offense is to take a walk through the scriptures in Genesis but before we go to Genesis an explanation of this chapter might be in order. When I began to write this chapter, specifically the first sentence, my Father immediately began speaking to me about forgiveness. This chapter was originally titled, "Offense", but is now, "Taking Offense and Giving Forgiveness". The two must go together in order to understand what each is and how they affect each other. So, before we dive into offense let's gain some understanding about forgiveness.

Low Cost High Dividends

Forgiveness is free when applied though faith in our Father. When forgiveness is given from our flesh sin nature it will always come with a cost, it will cost us some of our self, it never comes at the cost of others. It will cost you some pride perhaps or give you an opportunity to give up the right to justify yourself. Either way, by spirit or by flesh, forgiveness is a win-win. When we forgive someone or ask someone to forgive us, we release our God the Father, Creator of all things, to forgive us (Matthew 6:12,14,15). It brings cleansing, restoration and in some cases, it gives hope. Most importantly, though, when you involve forgiveness it always comes with God's love. It is by his love that forgiveness is given, and it is by his love that forgiveness is taken.

When the opportunity comes be willing to give forgiveness. When the opportunity comes be willing to take forgiveness when it is offered. The Power of forgiveness is immeasurable, it stretches across the heavens, it gave Jesus the ability to rise from the dead (Luke 23:34), and to preach the gospel to the dead. Be careful not to hold onto 'forgiveness' as this will only increase bad thoughts, self-pity, hatred, hurts, broken relationships and broken hearts. Holding onto forgiveness means you are not giving the situation over to the Father and you will be found to not be operating in trust. Yes, the hurts are real and the emotions are sometimes raw but we must remember He came to "…heal the broken hearted…" (Isaiah 61:1). Healing begins with humility, is processed though forgiveness, then completed with God's love.

Be quick to forgive. Be quick to repent. Be quick to allow God's love to bring peace. If you do not, then you will harden your heart and for what? Is not peace a more acceptable life than hurt or hatred? Is this not where offense rears its ugly head? Forgiveness is not about you it is about us, each and every one of us, who may be involved with that particular situation you are facing in your life. Because offense affects not just you but those close to you, your wife, your husband, your children, your parents, your best friends, your classmates, your co-workers, and on and on.

Offense is the ignition point for the likes of jealousy, anger, provocation, envy, or hatred. We have allowed ourselves to believe in the words spoken by another or the behavior of someone or our circumstances as we compare them to other people.

Offense is given and it is taken, but, if we do not *take* offense to what is said or the actions of another then we snuff out the ignition for all these other emotions or self-justifications. To take something is making an active acceptance of what was given. You are laying hold of it either physically or mentally. It is an action verb. Taking something that was not given is akin to stealing. But taking involves you making an action towards what was given. We are not able to control the thoughts or actions of another, but we certainly are responsible for our thoughts and actions (2 Corinthians 10:5). If we choose to take offense to what someone said or did then we give the right for jealousy or hatred or anger or envy or hurt feelings to run their course. Once this evil is conceived there is only one way for it to be overcome and that is forgiveness. The power behind forgiveness is love and that involves God because God is love. Choosing to take offense, if you are truly honest with yourself, is really your efforts to protect your-self, your way of thinking, justifying your actions and certainly not trusting the Most High God to provide, deliver, and change the hearts of those involved including your own.

Real Examples of Life

On to Genesis and the examples God has given us in the unfolding lives of Jacob and Esau. Exposing the deceit, offense, and forgiveness occurring in this family. God had promised his friend Abraham a son, whom Sarah his wife bore, naming him Isaac. Isaac and Rebekah fell in love giving birth to twins. The first born being Esau with Jacob following as the younger one. We will pick up the story in Genesis chapter 25.

Starting in verse 19 we have a short genealogy set up for us, as previously described, but Isaac's wife, Rebekah was barren – genealogies don't carry on very far if the next generation isn't being born. Isaac, on behalf of his wife, prays to God. The word for prayer here in Hebrew gives a meaning of intercession, entreating and supplication to God, who is waiting to listen.[4] God hears the intercession and entreating, and Rebekah conceives twins. How did she know she had twins? Because

---

[4] We do not know how or exactly what Isaac prayed, but he took the concern of his wife to the God who is waiting to listen. Because you may not always have an answer, or you may not understand why, doesn't mean you stop pouring your heart out to God. Isaac, as the authority over his wife, took the concern to God. We know that Rebekah communicated with God, as we will see later in this story, for she also entreated the Lord since she was the authority about what was going on in her womb. Both were willing to take the matters in their life that needed direction to the God who listens.

they struggled within her and a woman is acutely aware of how a pregnancy is affecting her body.

Rebekah goes to God to find out why they are struggling within her. God answers, "…you have two nations in your womb." Two peoples, two groups with similar bonds amongst their kinsmen. Esau, born first, red all over and very hairy, rather earthy in nature, who grew to be a hunter. The kind of guy who loved the outdoors, working the ground and hunting. Jacob, born second, being a peaceful man, living in tents, learning how to cook, yet having a grip with his hand on Esau's heel. What is the significance of this holding onto Esau's heel? It is a fulfilling of God's plan. God made two nations which would impact the Nation of Israel for years to come. The older son would serve the younger son and so it has always been. Jacob would be the one to supplant – trip up so to speak – his older brother, Esau.

Let's take a look at this family and what was happening on the home front by making a list.

1. Abraham was promised by God that he would be a father of many nations.
2. Esau and Jacob were born to Isaac, the child of promise, the son of Abraham.
3. Isaac, the Dad, loved Esau more than he did Jacob.
4. Rebekah, the Mom, loved Jacob more than she did Esau.
5. God was involved the whole time directing man's steps.

We have two brothers born together as twins yet each with completely different characters. Each parent having their favorite. Esau, however, was not willing to hold close the importance of the blessing and the inheritance as the right of the first born. While Jacob spent time in the tents thinking about those important things and how he might gain an upper hand.

The first event that sets in motion hard feelings between the boys has to do with the first born and his birthright. During these times this was important since it dealt with inheritance and the Father's blessing. Esau was out in the fields doing his thing and was out there long enough to get very hungry. Jacob was in the tent cooking up a pot of stew. In walks Esau from the field seeing this pot of red stew and asks his brother if he may have some of that, "red stuff", because he was, "famished." A typical outdoors man generally doesn't pay attention to the things going on at home thinking only about what is affecting him right now as he interacts with the outdoors.

Jacob, who obviously spent some time thinking about this, says "You must do this one thing before you can eat, Sell me your birthright." This isn't a knee jerk reaction; he didn't just come up with this. Was it wrong for Jacob to come up with this? It wasn't his to have he was born second. The birthright belonged to the firstborn. What was the purpose behind this thought? What did Jacob see in his brother Esau that would prompt such a proposal? Esau's response confirms his lack of respect for his inheritance and blessing. Genesis 25:32 says, "…I am at the point to die: and what profit shall this birthright do to me?"

Well, first we know that while they were in their Mother's womb, they struggled with each other, so being at odds with each other wasn't a new thing (Genesis 25: 22). Second, we know that Jacob's name labeled him as a supplanter, and he is living up to his name. Third, Jacob knew his brother and the way he thought about things, how he put importance on the things of the outdoors, hunting, and eating with his Dad.

Esau thought so little of the importance of his birthright that he was willing to give it up for a bowl of soup. God tells us that Esau despised his birthright (Hebrews 12:16; Genesis 25:34). If he did not despise or think so little of its value, he would not have sold it for a bowl of soup. God knew how little Esau would regard his birthright and He also knew Jacob would eventually seek Him and be changed.

The years passed when it came time for Isaac to pass on the blessing to his eldest son, he suggested to Esau to go hunting for game so Isaac could have something to eat before they got down to business. Isaac's wife, Rebekah, overheard the conversation and began to hatch a plan for her younger son, Jacob. It is important, here, to see this event, not like some mythical grand Biblical story, but see it like a family that faces life the same way families of today face life.

The perspective here is that Isaac loved Esau more because Isaac liked to eat the game that Esau would bring home, so before the blessing let's eat. The perspective here is that Rebekah loved Jacob more because he enjoyed doing those things she did living in the tent cooking. Mothers sometimes see things in their children the rest of us can't. *But* the difference in perspectives is she had heard from God that the two boys would lead two different nations and the older would serve the younger (Genesis 25:23). Rebekah was placing into motion what God had already established.

Rebekah calls Jacob and tells him to go prepare two of the kids from the flock, and she would prepare it for Isaac (Genesis 27: 9). You may ask why Jacob didn't cook it, possibly because she is the one who knew how to prepare it the way Isaac loved it, this way Isaac would be less suspecting.

You see, this isn't about some guy who flippantly gave up his birthright over a simple meal, no, it was much more. When we look at Hebrews 12: 16-17, we find Esau was immoral, profane, which is the same as being godless. Esau gave up the right of inheritance, which is what God set as an example of His relationship with those who believe that He is. The Greek words here in these verses really tend towards going across a threshold, in other words, stepping through a door as a decisive act. Esau made a decisive act to satisfy his appetite instead of clinging to God's inheritance as a son. This is, then, a rejection of God Himself. This now becomes a godless, profane, and immoral act. Any action taken that breaks from God as the author and finisher becomes an immoral act. Esau gave away his right to inheritance that comes from God. He took the wrong action and gave away the wrong thing.

Jacob may have been a supplanter in his approach to obtaining the birthright, but he knew what position this put him in with God. When Esau sought the blessing that comes with the birthright with loud crying, no repentance at this point would avail him.

Is this not a snapshot of judgement? When Jesus comes again to judge us all and we have been found to reject God's salvation, all our repentance with tears will not be accepted at this point. Now is a good time to repent and ask for His salvation, not later (2 Corinthians 6:2).

What was Esau's reaction to Isaac blessing his brother Jacob instead of him? He was not a happy camper, look at Genesis 27:41, "And Esau hated Jacob because of the blessing." Possibly Esau hated it because he was angry at himself for doing a foolish thing. He didn't seem to be interested in the inheritance when he was famished, but he certainly was longing for that blessing now. The blessing didn't come by itself. It came with the inheritance. You have to have the one before you get the other. His desire to receive the good outweighed his love for family, i.e., inheritance. His self-seeking thoughts led him to the deep emotion of hatred. Who was at fault here? At this point doesn't this sound like a good question? Well, this is how offence works, it wants you to give somebody the fault. Both had acted inappropriately in their decisions and actions so finding fault is useless. Forgiveness is willing to *take* the fault and say, "I'm sorry. Please forgive me."

Cain and Abel had a similar encounter, remember, Cain's sacrifice was rejected, and God had respect to Abel's offering. Cain became angry and instead of doing good (asking God for forgiveness) he allowed the offence to deepen his emotion of anger into hate. When the offence is consummated with the uncontrolled anger, death followed.

Esau was so offended he hated his brother, but the boys Mom showed some motherly wisdom and thought it best to separate the two. She sent Jacob off to visit her side of the family hoping in a short time Esau would cool down. The short time ended up being twenty years. During that time Jacob called upon God, dreamed dreams about the heavenlies, wrestled with God, was treated unfairly multiple times by family, humbled multiple times and even received a name change from Jacob to Israel. Through all the opportunities to take offence he remained submitted to God's blessing, bestowed by his father Isaac, which was a continuation of the promise given to Abraham by the Covenant established by God, taken on by Isaac then given to Jacob.

Both brothers had twenty years to work on their attitudes, do some growing up, and move on in life. Both had become successful in business and had many children, flocks, and camels. Jacob leaves his mother's family and sends messengers to Esau to let him know he is coming back home. Jacob in Genesis 32:7 reveals the depth of the conflict that occurred between him and his brother 20 years earlier. O, how things of the past can sometimes haunt us for years when offences are not dealt with. Jacob heard back from his messengers that Esau was coming with 400 men and he became, "…greatly afraid and distressed." Offence finds its strength in fear but remember forgiveness has its roots in love. When the two finally come together love won out over fear, they fell on each other's neck and kissed. You may ask, "When did Jacob ask Esau to forgive him?" When Jacob sent his messengers to Esau to explain where he has been and what has occurred in his life. In Genesis 32:5 Jacob wants to know if he found favor or grace in the eyes of his brother. Jacob wants to know if twenty years were enough to erase hatred.

Sometimes the opportunity to give forgiveness does not present itself for a long time and it is not that forgiveness doesn't present itself it is what we do with ourselves in the meantime. Esau apparently, during this time, eased in his hatred of his brother. While Jacob, during this time, learned more about God and the covenant promise passed down through his family. The question here, again, is what are we doing with ourselves during this time before the opportunity to give or take forgiveness presents itself? Are we harboring hatred or fear or despising another person for what was said or done? Are we growing and moving on or being held back in the past? Are we learning more about God, about Jesus, about the Holy Spirit and the covenant promise to the children of God? One way will lead us to a life not ruled by emotions, free of the past, and into a life that is more mature and self-controlled while the other path will lead us to bondage, frustrations, not lending itself to happiness and missing opportunities to enjoy and live free.

In Philippians 3 we read of Paul wanting to win Christ, to know Christ, to have the faith of Christ and attaining to the resurrection of the dead and how does he come about this? By not thinking he has already apprehended all of this but by doing this one thing we read in verse 13, "...forgetting those things which are behind, and reaching forth unto those things which are before." (Philippians 3:13). Paul has not boasted about apprehending or taking ahold of all these things of Christ. Instead he worked on forgetting the past with all of its failures, hurts, successes, and offenses and taking the forgiveness of Christ to live in His righteousness. When you forget about these things you are removing the opportunity to think or ponder on that offense. As your mind no longer recalls that offense it frees your heart to be filled with God's righteousness instead of fears, angers, and hatreds. Jacob, by involving forgiveness with Esau, was able to forget those things which are behind and this brought healing and restoration.

This chapter in no way gives the entire depth and meaning of offense, in fact, it barely starts the conversation. Offense has a book of its own, detailing who offends, how it is a stumbling block, how it causes sin and even the impact it has had on history. From wars, the rise and fall of nations and peoples, to the cross of Christ, offense has affected everyone – no person has not been touched by offense save for one – the man Jesus the Christ. Even he had moments where offense presented itself to him. How did he handle the offense people had towards him? By not bringing a railing accusation against them, by personally forgiving them, and asking the Father in Heaven to forgive them. This is the greatest act of forgiveness ever extrapolated upon mankind. The Creator of something forgiving that which He has created so He may

30

regain, reestablish, relationship and fellowship with them. John 3:16, "For God so loved the world that he *gave...*" He gave his Son, he gave forgiveness, he gave salvation, he gave us his Spirit, the Comforter, he gave everlasting life, he gave love, he gave man the antidote to offense, he gave forgiveness.[5]

Take what God has given. Take forgiveness it brings healing and restoration. Ask yourself if what you took offense to in the scheme of a lifetime is it really worth it? Please give God's love through forgiveness the chance to mend your brokenness. Stop with the self-justification. Stop with trying to protect your emotions and misunderstandings. Forgiveness demonstrates maturity. Forgiveness strengthens relationship. Forgiveness destroys bad attitudes and thoughts. Forgiveness gives renewal and freshness to your life.

Offense, or forgiveness, they are a choice. If you choose to take offense do you see the price you will have to pay and is it worth it? If you choose forgiveness do you trust the Most High God with your heart allowing him to contend with the situation bringing restoration and healing? The path of love is far less costly and far more rewarding.

---

[5] Psalm 119:165 reads, "Great peace have they which love thy law: and nothing shall offend them." The center column reads instead of offense, "they shall have no stumbling block." When you are filled with the love of God you gain understanding of who you are in Christ and the things of this world do not cause you to stumble. You have learned to trust in the One who created you in love and not to trust in a world that has fallen into a curse and sin and death. Forgiveness becomes the ladder that allows you to step over the stumbling block. Funny thing about stumbling, you may skin your knees or your hands or your elbows but you always have the right to get back up. When you do get up you learn to look for that stumbling block the next time you come across it and you will trust God, gain peace, and give and take forgiveness.

CHAPTER 4

GIVE AND TAKE OF HOPE, LOVE AND FAITH

That I may know Him and the Power of His resurrection…

-Philippians 3:10[6]

Hope

Such a part of every human that has walked the face of this earth. Not one person, ever, has not had hope in some form. From a simple child to those of age, hope has been in our lives. From ancient days to our present lives hope has been with mankind.

Who truly understands hope? Who hasn't spoken a prayer and it wasn't answered or at least not answered the way you thought it should be? Who hasn't hoped for something and, in this lifetime, not received it? Who hasn't had a dream dashed because of a hope that didn't happen?

Hope isn't something we should take lightly, hope is powerful. Hope is able to span generations, having lasting effects that impact the world. Yet we do take it lightly at times because we do not understand

---

[6] 1 Kings 8:60-61; "That all the people of the earth may know that the Lord is God, and that there is none else. Let your heart therefore be perfect with the Lord our God, to walk in his statutes, and to keep his commandments, as at this day.

the true depth that encompasses hope. Why do I say this? Well, look at the way we use it. We say simple things like, "I hope it doesn't rain for the game.", or "I hope you have a good time." Now clearly these are not wrong in themselves, but they lack the depth and understanding in the unassuming context of why we say them.

Let's turn to 1 Corinthians 13:13, "And now abide faith, hope and love…", These three are the most powerful aspects of the Christian life, the bedrock of our relationship with a Holy God. You may find these in different forms in other religions, but never in the unity and fullness that you have here. You will never find them in any other religion where it is the One true God that supplies them all, you cannot, on your own, fulfill them in this fulness. As you read this chapter you will see the power of faith, the involvement of hope, and the greatness of love.

Now, step back for a moment, take a deep breath and exhale slowly. Clear your mind and heart asking the Lord to open your heart to this. Now abides faith, hope, and love…, who is faith but our Lord Jesus (Hebrews 12:2), who is hope but the Holy Spirit (Romans 5:5), and who is love but God (1 John 4:16).

Faith is able to work on its own but without love (God) it rings hollow. Hope can be wished for but without love (God) it may or may not come to pass. Love without faith deters our victory (I John 5:4) and love without hope gives no vision beyond our current state. Hope without faith yields emptiness (Romans 4:18). The three may each stand on their own yet when they are one working together they bring fulfillment.

Hope, expectantly waiting in full assurance, is fueled by faith that calls those things that be not as though they were (Romans 4:17). Faith is fueled by knowing him and knowing him is discovering He is love, "That I may know him and the power of his resurrection." (Philippians 3:10).[7] This power is the love of God that gave us

---

[7] Expectantly waiting. You are not wishing, you are not wondering if it will happen, you are not saying this is what I hope for and turn around with a response to your

his only Son, the faith in that love to rise from the dead to give us a hope of salvation (1 Thessalonians 5:8). A hope that knows his love is good and in that knowing we are able to have vision that sees beyond (Psalm 9:10; Daniel 11:32; I John 5:11-13; 2 Peter 3:18).[8]

Abraham's Boldness

Abraham, in Genesis chapter 22, has received the child God has promised him, the child that was to translate into Abraham being the Father of many nations. But now God tells Abraham to, "Take your son and offer him as a sacrifice upon the altar." Abraham was instructed by God to take and give the life of the son he loved back to the God of Heaven. Genesis 22:4, "Then on the third day Abraham lifted up his eyes and saw the place afar off." Abraham had vision beyond the state he was in. He took his faith in that love of God that is so deep and powerful it is able to raise the dead to life and he wrapped it in a hope that knew that God would provide (Romans 4:17-18). He had vision that saw beyond the trial he was enduring, looking down through the centuries, and what he saw was Jesus being sacrificed on the very mount he had his son Isaac on (John 8:56). Abraham clung to the promise God had given him, God has given us a hope of eternal life (Titus 3:7). [9]

own statement saying it will probably never happen for me, no, you are expecting it. It is not going to happen, it has happened, maybe not in this moment or not in the next 20 years, but it has happened. This is knowing. This is trust. This is giving to God complete confidence that He is and what He has said has come to pass. Abraham expectantly waited 25 years for the child of promise by the God who could swear by no other because there is no other that is forever faithful, forever true and forever just.

[8] Hosea 6:3,6. Tells us we must follow on to know God, it is his desire for us to know him. It is his desire for us to be merciful. We live to know him. It is what we have been created for. Relationship is formed first, fellowship follows, and this is where we come to know Him, through personal fellowship.

[9] Philippians 3:14, "I press toward the mark for the prize of the high calling of God in Christ Jesus." Paul simply states in chapter 3:8 that the "...excellency of the knowledge of Christ Jesus my Lord...", is worth losing this life and what is so highly esteemed by this world. To know him. To know him. To know him. What joy, what life we would find if we would humble ourselves as our Lord did on his way to the cross, (Philippians 2:7-8). Abraham knew God had promised a child and God does not break promises,

So, where does this leave us? Down through the centuries hope has been discussed, written about, became notable quotes from very notable people, and even given up on by some. We tend to usually see only our own little lives, our troubles and distresses, our desires, our accomplishments and magnify them because this is what affects us. If you study some of the things written and said about hope you will find those who cling to it to sustain themselves through difficult times. You will also find those who believe it is best to forfeit hope, just moving on in life and doing those things that you need to do to accomplish what you want. Either way hope is still involved.

If you happen to fall into the latter category and you see hope as an unnecessary emotion, that good ole hard work is what pays the dividends, you are still functioning under hope. Hard work may help you produce things, this is true, but if I, for example, want to lift 150 pounds of weight over my head and I have never done it then it would behoove me to put in a little practice. I would start out with a lighter weight and work my way up to the set goal. Now when you start out you expect to achieve your goal or more. When you wait, expecting something to be accomplished, you are functioning in hope. Whether it is doing a physical workout to achieve a result, or starting your own business, or even composing a new song. We simply do not comprehend the depths that accompany hope. The broken promises we encounter here in this life, the dashed dreams, the life experiences that formulate our thinking all fall short of the glory of God. In order to harvest the hope that is full and sweet and complete we need to know him. We need to know him as our Father, as his Son our Savior, and as his Holy Spirit our counselor. The three working together as one for our good. Hope is integral with the drive that produces success. It is what keeps us going, sustains us, when it doesn't appear to be going as we would like it to. It gives us strength to endure hardness and overcome.

---

no matter what it looks like on this world. Abraham saw, or perceived, what God had planned by the fulfilling of faith to all generations.

Well, you say, that sounds good, but you know nothing about how bad my marriage is, or maybe how no one encourages me, they all make fun of me. You might be someone who lives in a country that demonstrates persecution against you for your religion or your political beliefs. Possibly you come from nothing, scarcely scratching out an existence, living day to day at best. It could be you have everything money can buy yet feel like an empty shell. Perhaps a great tragedy has struck you or your loved ones. This list can go on and on, you know where you are at and what is happening in your life, don't you?

It seems, for some, what they have hoped for has come true and that is like a medicine, for others it seems like there is no hope left (Proverbs 13:12; 17:22). How do you make sense of all this? By knowing him. If you know him then you are approaching life with less about yourself and more about the love he has for you. It doesn't happen all at once, giving up yourself, having a faith that knows his love, it takes times and seasons and trials. If not for the struggles, what would we become? If not for the hardships, if not for the persecutions, if not for the harassments, injustices, accusations, setbacks, lies and put downs how would we know we are trusting him with our growth, with our faith, with our deliverance from evil. Do not succumb to these as they are not what God made you to be but simply use them as a tool to turn you to the knowledge of Christ, of obedience, of less of you and more of him.

We depend upon ourselves a great deal which can lead us into a false hope. We hope for something not knowing the impact it may have upon us or even upon someone we don't even know yet. His perfect love knows our path. The path to proper hope is through faith in a Creator that is the beginning and the ending. A faith that knows him and the power of his resurrection. A love that gives. A hope that waits expectantly.

If you are the one who believes in hard work to accomplish what you want, then work hard, but don't leave out faith and love. When, and if, you accomplish what you set yourself to do, don't take the glory, because he is still God and every good gift comes from above. (James 1:17; John 19:11-12). For what does it profit a man if he were to gain the whole world yet lose his own soul (Matthew 16:26)?

Let's take a look again at Abraham from the time God promised he would be the father of many nations to the time Sarah, his wife, brought forth her first born, Isaac, it was 25 years. That is a long enough time for doubt to occur (Romans 4:17-21). Hope and faith, however, never ceased with Abraham. He didn't stagger at the promise God gave him.

Well, you say, I am not Abraham and that is true, you are not Abraham in person, but you are his in the heritage of faith (Romans 4:16; Hebrews 6:11-15). God made a covenant with Abraham and since there is no one greater, God swore by two immutable things, 1. It is impossible for God to lie and, 2. Jesus was made a high priest who became the sacrifice for our sins (Romans 6:17-20). This is the promise given to all of us – eternal life through Jesus Christ His Son. This is what Abraham saw on the mount with his son Isaac. Faith is what makes it available to us today. Started by God, made covenant with Abraham, finished with the resurrection of Jesus and ours through faith.

Take time to read 2 Peter 1:2-9. You will find here that in knowing him, we are able to take hold of his promise. But, if we don't choose faith, hope and love while grabbing hold of his promise we will have a blindness. If you think this is all a bunch of folly just look around you. When you see someone who is touched by love and hope after a tragedy, where do you think this comes from? A blind person cannot see the sunlight, yet they are able to feel its warmth. If you do not know him, you still recognize love and hope when it comes along. What you do with it is your choice. Remember, Jesus, whether you choose to believe him or not, you must admit that the world has most certainly been impacted by the hope, the faith, and the love that has sprung forth from this man.

The Intensity of Ruth

Take a look at another example for us in the book of Ruth. There was a man named Elimelech with his wife Naomi and their two sons coming from Bethlehem-Judah. A famine in the land caused him to move his family to another country. While there Elimelech passed away leaving his wife and two sons. The sons ended up taking wives now it was Naomi, her two sons, and her daughters-in-law. At some point both of her sons passed away as well. Here is Naomi, having lost her husband, both of her sons, living in a strange land, leaving only her and her two daughters-in-law. She has no family to draw upon for her daughters-in-law, so she told them to move back to their own mothers. This is real – this is life – even for today. Now look at how deep this hurt goes, turn to chapter 1:9, the hurt was deep because the love was deep. Naomi kissed them, they all wept. Finally, after much prodding one daughter-in-law, Orpah relents and went back to her land and her mother's house. But, Ruth, the other daughter-in-law, made a stand, a commitment, "Where you go, I go, where you live, I live, your people shall be my people and your God my God." (Ruth 1:16 paraphrased).

Ruth and Naomi return to Bethlehem-Judah to live from the gleaning of what has been leftover in the fields after the harvest. This is tough. This isn't what most of us consider the good life. This is hardship. Even Naomi has run out of hope. But, Ruth's decision to trust God (Ruth 2:12), is about to reap the benefits of faith, hope, and love.

Naomi and Ruth's return seemed to be in brokenness, but God brought them to the place where inheritance existed. Ruth met Boaz, who is a kinsman of Naomi. Boaz and Ruth get married, giving birth to a son (Ruth 4:13-15), which brought blessing and honor to Naomi. At multiple points in Ruth's life there was opportunity for doubt, for thinking this simply isn't working out and it is too difficult for me to carry on but instead she exhibited intensity and determination of faith that wouldn't let go of the God she claimed to be her God. This story in itself is, at worst, inspirational, but at its best, this child born to Boaz and Ruth, became the father of Jesse, who happened to be the father of David, who became King of Israel and whose lineage Jesus came from all through God's plan and promises (Ruth 4:17). That same intensity surely passed down the lineage to David because he most certainly demonstrated an intense faith.

In our brokenness, in our confusion, in our misunderstandings, in our anger and even in our successes, we need hope, we need faith and we need love. Life on this earth will always have its challenges, its victories, and its failures. Life is continuous, it is happening every day to all of us. For some, it will be easier than for others. By knowing him and by giving up the right to ourselves, taking up dependence upon him, we begin to see as he sees, to know as he knows and to love as he loves.

What we may see as evil he is able to bring about as good. Our hurts can disappear in his love. [10]

Knowing: If we know Him, We will love Him.

If we love Him, We will Know Him

"Behold, what manner of love the Father has bestowed upon us, that we should be called the children of God: therefore, the world *knows* us not, because it *knew* Him not." (1 John 3:1 KJV).

Jesus said, "But I *know* you, that you have not the love of God in you." (John 5:42 KJV).

In the book of 1 John, (KJV), the word "know" is used thirty-one times in five chapters and 105 verses. This word is described as, "to

---

[10] Jeremiah 31:17, "There is hope in your future…". If we don't live in hope, then we are missing one of the most fundamental realities and truths about the God of all hope. Do you really think you are just ambling along in this existence? He has given us hope to help us cope with a sinful world. Hope directed through God brings us something this world refuses to offer. Romans 15:13, "Now the God of Hope fill you with all joy and peace as you *believe* in Him, so that you may *overflow* with hope by the power of the Holy Spirit." (Bible Hub Berean Study Bible).

have seen or perceived, hence, to know.", (Strong's 3609 HGKSB). This book of I John is about what we know, what we don't know, what we should know, what proof he has given us and what we need to do to take what he has given. And it is all about his love.

What do we know about His love? If we don't love one another, if we don't love our brother, if we don't love our neighbor then we don't know him (reference John 5:42 above).

Love is the innocence of a child. If you are a father or mother and you have held your baby in your bosom while they sleep, you are experiencing the simple innocent trust that comes from love.

In Proverbs 8:17, Wisdom is telling us, "I love them that love me; and those that seek me early shall find me." Seeking wisdom through the fear of the Lord by hating evil, pride and arrogancy (Proverbs 8:13) will bring us into Wisdom's love. Jesus is our wisdom, he has always been, and he loves those who are willing to love him.

Love is simple and innocent as stated above. It is not complicated or difficult, it is pure and always fresh. God is the great, "I Am", which means He is always right now, whether that be in the past, present or future. Since God is love, His love is always right now, regardless of where you've been or where you are, or where you are going. Jesus didn't come to judge or complicate love. He came *because* he loved us. This is wisdom and we know we love him if we keep his commandments (1 John 3:23; 4:10-11; John 15:10).

Jesus wants us to come to him in that simple childlike love and rest upon his bosom, trusting him with our very lives. Knowing that the Holy Spirit is given to us because we love Him, and He loves us. I John 4:16, "And we have *known* and believed the love that God has to us. God is love and he that dwells in love dwells in God, and God in Him."

Do you know who God is? He is the One who is patient, suffering a long time for us to grow in fellowship with him. He is the One who is kind bestowing upon us great mercies. He is the One who is not envious of what we have or who we are. He is the One who has no arrogancy and does not brag about what he has done. He does not act unbecoming or foolishly. He is not selfish seeking only for his own self-justification or promotion. He is the One who is not easily provoked by our disobedience. He is the One who does not think on evil for if he did He would be thinking contrary to who he is. He is the One who does not rejoice in a sinful nature, but he sure does rejoice with truth because he is Truth. He alone is able to bear all things. He alone is able to believe all things. He alone is able to hope all things which gives us an expected end to our days. He alone is the One who is able to endure by remaining under our miseries, our adversities, our persecutions, our prejudices, our conflicts, and our shortcomings. He stays. He does not desert us through these distresses. He never fails. Love is who He is (Ref. 1 Corinthians 13).

What do we do here at this point? Most of us scarcely know love, well, the true depth of it at least. Some have experienced enduring love, like my parents who have been married over 70 years. Some have ever-so-brief-yet-precious-beyond-words love, such as those who may have lost a baby in their early days. Some have experienced passionate love. Some have had strong love while some have had little love. Some have had love that stayed during the struggles. The more we live and experience love, the more we come to know the God of love, even during the struggles, the losses, the disciplines, the exuberance, and the passions. We may not recognize it is his love that is always there to comfort, grow and strengthen us but it is always his love.

What we do here at this point is no matter how much love or how little love we may have experienced is we just never give up on love, we never give up on its kindness, we never give up on its gentleness, we never give up on its hope, we never give up on its patience, we never give up on its endurance. We look not to ourselves, for pride when offended, leads to frustrations and anger, which allows emotions

41

to come out of balance. Instead, we behave ourselves in a manner of meekness. We believe the best and we don't think evil.

Hope, if it is true, is born out of love. What we hope for is that the God of love gives us understanding while we go through each situation or circumstance or event in life.

In all of this we give God the opportunity to love in our lives and, love, is never meant for just one it will always spread to others. All you have to do is give it away.

"And they shall teach no more every man his neighbour, and every man his brother, saying, Know the LORD: for they shall all know me, from the least of them unto the greatest of them, saith the LORD: for I will forgive their iniquity, and I will remember their sin no more." Jeremiah 31:34. When he forgives us through his love he no longer remembers our sin for if he kept it as a memory then it could at some occasion come back to him for him to think about and remember our falling short. How often do we think we forgive someone yet keep it in our memory? How often when a trouble comes it strikes that memory and we are caught back in the same unforgiveness and sin and doubt? Do you see how his love doesn't go there. Neither should we. By knowing him we know his love and it is so beautiful that it simply doesn't remember our iniquities because we have asked him to forgive us and his love does just that – it forgives. Now we are in his love and this is where our freedom truly exists. Imagine having a spirit that is free from unforgiveness and completely free in the life of love. Ask him for it he will give it through Jesus Christ.

Believing (Acting in Full Assurance)

We have hope, which expectantly waits in knowing him (John 14:4,6,7,9,17,18). We have love which is God himself. What is left then, but faith which works by love (Galatians 5:6). Not a law that burdens (Matthew 23:4) but a truth that makes us free.

Return to the book of Ruth with me and see what faith did for her. Ruth and Naomi were living their life every day just as we do today. Getting married, leaving the land they had grown up in, losing their husbands, just surviving the best they can. Thinking they had moved to a good life but now feeling empty and hurt (Ruth 1:21). They came back to Bethlehem, not in victory, but in brokenness and affliction. Naomi went so far as to be willing to change her name from Naomi which means Pleasant to Mara meaning Bitter (Ruth 1:20). A lot of hurt for a woman to bear in a life.

But stop a minute and look back on Ruth's confession before they decided to move back to Bethlehem, after she had lost her husband. She said do not ask me to leave you or return to my Mother. Because where you go, I go. Where you live, I will live. Your people shall be my people and your God shall be my God. Where you die is where I will die and be buried (Ruth 1:16-17). Even through the dark hours she confessed a desire to trust in Naomi's God. She settled the matter in her heart and soul, deciding to cling to relationship, inheritance, and fellowship.

This faith, this trust, saw beyond the darkness not getting caught up in the affliction but staying faithful, "…your God shall be my God." She continued to work, she continued to help her Mother-in-law and continued to trust. She accepted that Jehovah, God of Israel, was the one true God and that it is better to be considered a child of God then to be found without him.

The fruit of that faith resulted in her happening upon gleaning in the one field that belonged to Naomi's kinsman. Her faith being acted out by continuing to help Naomi, became a witness to her. Boaz, who was Naomi's kinsman, saw and heard of her diligence (Ruth 2:1). He knew God would be willing to give full reward because she had come to trust in Him in such a peaceful way, "Under whose wings thou art come to trust." (Ruth 2:12).

God had a plan in motion (because he spoke it out in the book of Genesis 3:15) that would lead to sending his Son to be a part of his creation. Luke 1:45 has Elizabeth speaking in the Holy Ghost to Mary the Mother of Jesus and declares Mary blessed for believing and this believing is the fulfillment of this plan. What our God speaks, he performs, it happens. Ruth may not have had a full knowledge of God's plan but that is where faith comes in. We don't know all the details, but we know him. We know he is love. We know that he is faithful to perform what he speaks. We know he will never leave us nor forsake us. We know he forgives us as we forgive others. We know that there is no other god like our God and that he is coming again in righteousness and judgement.

Faith has vision. Faith hears. Faith speaks the truth of My Promises says the Lord. Faith knows. Look here now, it is time to press on past these simple truths of faith we have been discussing on to the root of faith, to Jesus, the author and finisher of our faith (Hebrews 12:2).

Confidence in an established end to the purpose

Absolutely destroys fear and doubt

Fear and doubt left unchecked, in turn then,

Can destroy a vision.

Why is Jesus the author of faith? Why would the Son of a living God need faith? He authored faith to be made like unto his brethren (Hebrews 2:17-18). When Adam and Eve sinned in the Garden of Eden, they had up to this point only walked with God, they had not known life without Him. God knew man (the human race) would fall away from the presence of the Living God. No longer seeing or walking with God, faith would now be our access to Him.

Remember, previously, we discussed when Adam and Eve disobeyed God, death came upon us. From that time until now death has reigned upon mankind (1 Corinthians 15:21-22). Death to our physical, death in our thinking, death in our relationships, death in all things that pertain to man. Now enters fear. We fear death and because we fear death we do all manner of things to try to protect ourselves, to justify our lives, our actions, our thoughts. We turn truth into lies. We act violently because we don't understand. We don't commit because we are afraid of failure. We reject those things that seem contrary to ourselves. We judge because we wish to protect ourselves, to promote ourselves, all for emotional security.

Jesus was sent to be the reconciliation for the sins of the people to redeem us from the curse of death.

"But we see Jesus who was made a little lower than the angels by the suffering of death, crowned with glory and honor; that he by the grace of God should taste death for every man." Hebrews 2:9 KJV

Jesus is the triune God, the Son, the Word that was with God, that was God in the beginning (John 1:1-3). Hebrews 2:8 says that all things have been put in subjection under his feet. Jesus suffered death for everyone. Abraham saw this day and was glad, he rejoiced to see it (John 8:56). Remember he saw it when he was getting ready to sacrifice his own son, but God showed him that God himself would provide the sacrifice.

All things had been put in subjection under His feet except death. So, Jesus, became flesh and blood just like all of us (Hebrews 2:14) to experience the suffering of death. If we end it here in this death, if the dead rise not than there is nothing else, hope is for naught, love is for naught, forgiveness is for naught. Do what you please because you, yourself, may die tomorrow (1 Corinthians 15:32). There would only be you to live for. *But*, Hebrews 2:14 tells us, "…that through death he might destroy him that had the power of death, that is, the devil." How do you destroy death? By giving life! Jesus gave us life by rising from the grave. Whatever power and authority Satan had over mankind was taken from him by the death, burial, *and* resurrection. Jesus experienced the same death that we experience on this earth but by faith, he knew, that God is able to give life to the dead, he is able to overcome death (read 1 Corinthians 6:14).

Death is not to be feared. Death is to be used to our benefit. Physical death comes to us all and if we have confessed our sins to Him, asked for forgiveness, and believed in faith that He has saved us from death, knowing we shall rise with him then life is ours in Christ and we will stand in His presence (Colossians 3:3,4; Philippians 1:21-24).

"And deliver them who through fear of death were all their lifetime subject to bondage." (Hebrews 2:15).

"O death, where is thy sting? O grave, where is thy victory? The sting of death is sin; the strength of sin is the law. But thanks be to God, which gives us the victory through our Lord Jesus Christ." (1 Corinthians 15:55-57).

Jesus has given us victory over death we are not to be in bondage to death any longer. Remember, man's fall in Genesis brought death to our physical and this is easy for us to recognize since we see people die every day. But the death that came with the fall of man was much more than the physical, remember, Adam died in his relationship with God, he was no longer able to walk with God in the Garden. Death to our spirit is what happened we were no longer able to walk with God spiritually. What followed was death in our relationships with each other, death by our unforgiveness, death to our humility; which resulted in pride, death in faith; which resulted in a lack of the fear of the Lord, death in love; which resulted in a self-knowledge, causing us to not know that God is love.

But death is for our benefit. When we are born from above, we are now in life that is bought with a price (Revelation 5:9-10). 1 Corinthians 15:35-58 explains what death is, it is the path to life. When a seed is planted it doesn't stay that lone single seed, everything to succeed in life is already in that seed, it sprouts and grows but first it dies to what

46

it was in order to become more. Our physical, when born from above, will put on a new incorruptible life (Romans 8:10) as we become the body of Christ.

In 1 Corinthians 15:31 Paul the apostle states, "…I die daily." Now, we are talking about dying to self, the flesh sin nature, this is that corruptible seed dying so that new life can spring forth. Where unforgiveness dies, forgiveness lives. Where pride dies, humility lives. Faith sprouts and grows. Love sprouts and grows. We die daily that Christ may live in us and relationships may flourish. Death to ourselves, our flesh sin nature, is what allows this seed to become more, become new, become fruitful.

His love enables us to receive more. It is by and through his love that we are able to resist the devil, that we are able to take his promises, that we are allowed to go through the process of dying to ourselves so that we might gain Christ.

His love is life and it produces life. A dead seed will grow nothing. A live seed, when planted and watered, will grow and produce fruit which produces more life. Your spirit is dead and separated from the living God until you make that conscious decision to accept Jesus as your Savior.

At this point love comes in and makes your spirit alive. Now the growing process begins. You begin to develop a root that absorbs the nutrients from the Word of God. Drawing moisture from the Holy Spirit which flows through every fiber of your being shedding the love of God abroad in your heart. Your spirit cannot be alive without the Holy Spirit, who is life, who is love, because love begets life.

No living plant, no living human does not have a cell or any area that does not have moisture. As the roots draw moisture into the plant there is not one area that is dry. If any part of that plant has no water that part will die. If you have received Jesus the Christ as your Savior and you have a dry area you best be looking and asking God to reveal to you what is choking that life. Ask him to remove it by repenting and by taking in that living water of the Holy Ghost. Ah, such liberty to be free in the Spirit of God.

All those pressures you encounter in this life, all those hot dry days you experience in difficult circumstances, all those struggles that make you doubt or question or wonder if you are failing God or falling short or if you will even make it at all, all of these are simply the opportunities given us to draw on his love in faith and by faith. The less of you (and each seed must die to itself before it may grow) and the more of the fresh water of the Holy Spirit you absorb the greater the love in you. Remember it is love that overcame the world.

No seed ever questioned or complained about the hardness of pushing through the soil. No seed ever complained about the hot dry spells. So we, who complain about everything, should continually look to Jesus the Word. We should rely on and quietly listen to the Holy Spirit. We should at all times and in all conditions we encounter come boldly to the Throne of Grace where our Father sits and this is done in faith with an absolute knowing that he is love and our life springs from this love.

Are you getting it yet? Are you beginning to grasp the strength of faith? Faith does not mature in your flesh. Faith is a thing of the spirit. Faith is not what you see standing in front of you when your husband or son or wife or daughter are missing the mark following the things this world so deceptively offers. No, faith is looking beyond what you see standing in front of you because it sees God, in His love, moving heaven and earth to accomplish the faith you are actively speaking, knowing, and doing.

This death, burial and resurrection of Jesus gave us faith (Romans 12:3). We must live by faith. We must love by faith. We must grow by faith. We must believe that He is, by faith.

Hope, love, and faith; a final word

We must take this hope in patient expectancy, waiting on the Father to perform what He has promised us. We must take his faith that he has given us so that we may have vision beyond what we see here and now, knowing his will be done. We must take his love that he so lovingly, tenderly, graciously, kindly has bestowed upon us and give it away to our neighbor (a neighbor is anyone we have the opportunity to get to know and offer ourselves to as the need arises). By loving our neighbor, we fulfill God's law (Romans 13:8-10). Love is never intended to be wasted on selfishness.

Embrace them with your mind, soul, body, and spirit. Love the Lord with all your heart and with all your soul and with all your strength (Deuteronomy 6:5). Love is the foundation of hope. Faith is the fuel of hope and love is empowered by faith. God loves a faithful man. He gives hope so faith may continue to strengthen. The Trinity is involved here because he is the God of all Hope, the Holy Spirit sheds the love of God abroad in our hearts, and Jesus is the author and finisher of our faith. Believe it. Know it. Abide in it.

Give hope to encourage others. Take hope as needed to endure. Give faith the chance it needs to grow. Take faith that Jesus provides for us. Give love to conquer fear. Take love to live.

CHAPTER 5

WEAPONS OF WARFARE
OR
TAKE CAPTIVE THOUGHTS

"Come unto me, all ye that labor and are heavy laden, and
I will give you rest. Take my yoke upon you, and learn of me:
For I am meek and lowly in heart: and you shall find rest unto your
Souls. For my yoke is easy, and my burden is light."

- Mathew 11:28-30

Warfare and thoughts. You do not have one without the other. Our thoughts are the breeding ground for how we allow ourselves to perceive something, for the words we speak, for the decisions we make. Our thoughts can lift us up or tear us down. Our thoughts can be thoughts that lead to life and light or death and darkness. So, let's study what the word of God says about our thoughts and how they relate to our Creator and Savior.

Discover the Origin

Thoughts may originate in three separate arenas:

1.   God's thoughts.

Jeremiah 29:10-11 reads, "…I will visit you, and perform my good word toward You, in causing you to return to this place. For I know the thoughts that I *think* toward you, saith the Lord, thoughts of peace, and not of evil, to *give* you an end and expectation [center column].

Isaiah 55:8-11 reads, "For my thoughts are not your thoughts, neither are your ways my ways, saith the Lord. For as the heavens are higher than the earth, so are my ways higher than your ways, and my thoughts than your thoughts. For as the rain cometh down, and the snow from heaven, and returneth not thither, but watereth the earth, and maketh it bring forth and bud, that it may *give* seed to the sower, and bread to the eater: So shall my word be that goeth forth out of my mouth: it shall not return to me void, but it shall accomplish that which I please, and it shall prosper in the thing whereto I sent it."

2.   Our self-thoughts.

Genesis 11:6 reads, "And the Lord said, Behold, the people is one, and they have all one language; and this they begin to do: and now nothing will be restrained from them, which they have imagined to do." (or purposed in their thoughts).

Isaiah 55:7 reads, "Let the wicked forsake his way, and the unrighteous man his thoughts: and let him return unto the Lord, and he will have mercy upon him: and to our God, for he will abundantly pardon."

Romans 1:28 reads, "And even as they did not like to acknowledge God (center column) in their knowledge, God gave them over to a mind void of judgement (center column) to do those things which are not convenient:"

Mathew 16:7 reads, "And they reasoned among themselves, …"

Luke 20:5 reads, "And they reasoned with themselves, saying, If we shall say, From heaven: he will say, Why then believed ye him not?"

Mark 2:8 reads, "And immediately when Jesus perceived in his spirit that they so reasoned within themselves, he said unto them, Why reason ye these things in your heart?

3.   Satan's interjections.

John 8:44 reads, "Ye are of your father the devil, and the lusts of your father ye will do. He was a murderer from the beginning, and abode not in the truth, because there is no truth in him. When he speaketh a lie, he speaketh of his own: for he is a liar, and the father of it."

Genesis 3:13 reads, "And the Lord God said unto the woman, What is this that thou hast done? And the woman said, The serpent beguiled me, and I did eat."

God's thoughts always succeed, they accomplish what they were set out to perform, they produce life. Our self-thoughts promote us. They draw attention to us whether in self-pity, suicide, glorifying our accomplishments, demeaning someone else or promoting ourselves to cover up our insecurities.[11] Thoughts injected by Satan will always lead to death. Death of relationships between each other, between us and the promises of the Creator and between us and the success of everlasting life. Thoughts from Satan are bound by lies and exist through deception.

God's thoughts show up in the beginning, take a look at Genesis 1 where God is creating the heavens and the earth, He creates something, stops, takes a look at it, and says, "that is good." Genesis 1:4, "And God *saw* that the light was good: and God separated the light from

---

[11] In doing the will of the Father, it never comes at the cost of others, it always comes at the cost of self. When you think, (take a thought), you deserve something, you are promoting your "self". God is not in self, (our flesh, sin nature), God is Spirit, and this is where we worship Him. In Spirit. Worshiping in Spirit is doing the will of the Father.

the darkness." The Hebrew word for "saw" is repeated in chapter one, seven times. This is also the same word given in chapter 3:6, "When the woman *saw* that the tree was good…".

So, what does this have to do with our thoughts? The Hebrew rendering for this word is defined as to see, to perceive, to understand, etc. This is gaining an intellectual perception, a formulating of thoughts, concerning something (HGKSB, Strong's 7200 O.T. *Raah* NASB). Here God is thinking on what He spoke and seeing it was accomplished and that it was good. The woman, however, wasn't just thinking this is a good-looking fruit, she was drawing a perception that eating of this fruit from the Tree of the Knowledge of Good and Evil would establish that she could be more than she already was. She knew the truth yet allowed herself to be deceived by not capturing the thought that was a lie given to her by the Serpent. Formulating or gaining intellectual understanding is completely influenced by not only what we take in as we see, hear, speak, and experience, but by how we dwell on those thoughts, and by what arena we desire to give the prominence to. The arena of God's thoughts bring life, the arena of our thoughts promote self, and the arena of Satan's thoughts cause death.

You see, if God is thinking about things (and we are made in His image) then thought is every bit as much a part of us. It is how things happen, how they get accomplished. We give it a thought. We are also able to take a thought. We may take a thought captive, or we may give into a lie, a deception. You are responsible for which arena you desire to draw from. You may believe the truth or twist it to render the thoughts so that you feel comfortable with them. Just so you know, God does not always concern Himself about how comfortable you feel. He most certainly is concerned with what you have in you that hinders the growth of the Word, the Spirit, and the life He has for you.

Our Heart and Rebellion

At this point we need to clarify a couple of items here. One, what our heart is, and two, what is rebellion, because both of these have much to do with our thoughts.

Our heart is essentially who we really are, our inner most being. That central part of us that is multifaceted to include our emotions, our will, our hurts, our strengths, and our individuality. It includes our mind which is the search engine for our thoughts. This is how God set us up when He created us, but we have the ability to add to it by what we think, by how we perceive a thing. As we grow up from a child, we are exposed to innumerable experiences that require thought. Some experiences are good, some are hurtful, some excite us, some are overwhelming, some are life changing and some we don't even give a thought about. No matter what the experience, the thoughts we give toward that experience, the thoughts we take from that experience all have a direct influence on our heart, who we really are.[12]

Rebellion, what a powerful word as it is an action of the heart and what your mind is taking in. It is often used today with little emphasis on how strong this word really is. People call themselves a rebel today when really all they are is disobedient for selfish reasons, immature in their nature.

Rebellion is simply knowing the authority, knowing the rules, and deciding to not follow them. In the Hebrew it "gives the impression of being disobedient towards someone, to be refractory, to resist, to despise, to quarrel, to dispute or to offend. Literally it means to be or

---

[12] Even though we have the ability to add to our experiences through our thoughts, it is still God who fashions our hearts because he always gives us a choice – choose life or choose death. A choice cannot be made without giving or taking a thought. Psalm 33:15, "He fashions their hearts alike; he considers all their works." 2 Chronicles 16:9, "For the eyes of the LORD roam to and fro over all the earth, to show Himself strong on behalf of those whose heart is fully devoted to Him." Job 34:21, "For His eyes are on the ways of man, and He sees his every step."

make bitter or unpleasant. Provoking a situation becomes an inherent component of this term" (HGKSB, Strong's 4784 *Marah*). [13]

The scriptures are full of terms, examples and descriptions concerning the heart and rebellion. From God's thoughts concerning creation to created man thinking about himself to Satan thinking about stealing man's inheritance through lies. From the Israelites provoking God in the wilderness to Goliath defying the Israelite armies. Even Jesus spoke about what comes out of a man's heart is what defiles him (Matthew 15:18-19). This entire existence of man on this planet has been one of, by choice, a rebellious mindset turning from the life, grace, love, power, blessing, successes, and presence of the only one who is able to create such intricate, delicate, intertwined nature, relationships, sciences, mathematics, and undiscovered intellectual capacities. How we think about the things we encounter on this earth is far more important than we would give credit to.

The Flesh Thoughts

It is easy for us to recognize which arena thoughts are being generated in. As previously stated in this book while in the Garden Adam and Eve were both naked before God and each other (nothing to hide) and had not experienced the failure of sin. There was nothing to be ashamed of or confused by. But they spoke with the adversary and began to *take* thoughts, which, when allowed to be conceived, bring forth sin consciousness in man. They did not apply the Spoken Word of God as told in Genesis 2:16-17, utilizing God's instructions and

---

[13] Proverbs 4:23, "Keep thy heart with all diligence; for out of it are the issues of life." If you were to study this verse and the renderings of these words in the Greek, the Latin and the Hebrew, you would gain a greater understanding of the importance of your thoughts and how they affect your life, health, relationships, and endeavors. You are to take an active responsibility to keep or guard with all diligence, making a real effort, to concern yourself with what is in your heart. A heart based on or filled with truth is like a mountain spring that breaks forth from the rocks, it flows, it escapes from its source. It is life giving, it is raw, it is strong, it is refreshing. It is what gives power to life.

covering. They chose to, or *refused to make* the proper decision; therefore, their hearts (the whole spectrum of human thought, emotions, wisdom, and understanding, their will, the totality of their inner nature) were hardened towards God's command of protection. Their refusal to make a proper decision led to the beginning of a hardened heart. This is being rebellious. They became disobedient toward God, resistant, refractory, defiant! This led to a lack of wisdom and understanding.[14]

Now that we have a consciousness of sin, it reveals our relationship with God to be broken. Now it manifests itself in the actions of the spirit of the heart to be good or evil, righteous, or unholy, faith or doubt. Being aware of what is evil and what is good in our relationship with each other and in our relationship with God. By His forgiveness we no longer have to have an awareness of sin committed, but, an awareness of the mind of Christ. A mind of obedience through suffering. A mind of humility. A mind of a giving love. A mind of forgiveness with each other. A mind of mercy. A mind of kindness. A mind of patience. A mind of endurance. A mind of peace. A mind of compassion. A mind of instruction. A mind of the Word with God. A mind of faith. A mind of hope of eternal life. A mind of inheritance. A mind of power, of love and a sound mind. This is what He has given to us when we repent and receive His forgiveness of sin.

This is where we enter warfare in the battle to renew our mind. Romans 1:19 tells us we already know God is, we have no excuse. So, what has happened? We made choices to let go of truth and we made choices to be deceived. When we listen to lying and deceiving spirits, continually absorbing these into our minds it soon enters our hearts and we fall away from the faith that knows and believes in a God of love. This is the point where hatred overtakes us. Where anger builds because we now think we must justify ourselves, our moral conscience. When we see evils perpetrated upon each other by rape or murder, by

---

[14] Understanding is a heart given to God which is the ability to apply wisdom. When you know Jesus as your Savior, you have found wisdom because Jesus is wisdom. The same wisdom that was with God in the beginning (1 Corinthians 1:30; John 1:1,2).

stealing or by imposing our thoughts upon another relieving them of their freedoms to act, or by giving ourselves; our moral conscience, over to demonic control of our thoughts for the sole purpose of destruction of others, of our leaders, and even of nations, then we have lost the battle and for some maybe even the war.

God Thoughts

But you need to realize our God is a consuming fire. Nothing is hid that shall not be revealed (Luke 12:2). Your ill-conceived thoughts, hatred, anger, and desires are not bigger than the Most High God. By turning to God in repentance He is willing to redeem us from this curse. *No Matter What!*

What we must remember is, He is our Lord, our Savior, Creator of heaven and earth. Everything we judge, everything we set our opinions on, everything we set ourselves above in vain pride comes from our heart, the center of us filled by the thoughts and intents of our heart. Jeremiah 4:22 tells us we are foolish because we have not known him, that we are shrewd or wise to do evil (life without dependence upon God) but to do good, we do not know.

God's thoughts are the parable of the sower, sowing seed in all places, giving all of us the chance to choose how they receive the word of God. God's thoughts are of peace. God's thoughts are of hope and prosperity (Jeremiah 29:11). God gives promises. Promises are spoken thoughts concerning what you intend to accomplish (2 Peter 1:4). God establishes covenant. He spoke it over Noah and his sons, setting a reminder in the sky, so every time he sent a rainstorm, and the rainbow, no matter where it would appear on the earth, he would remember the covenant he established between man and every living creature (Genesis 9:8-17). Would you think it wise to take lightly a promise from the living God or to disregard a covenant He established with you? Be careful how you handle His promises and His covenants. Do not spin them to fit your sinful nature. Surely, he sees us, what we do, what we think. Self-justification of your desires, thoughts, actions and fulfilling of your sinful nature's satisfaction do not go unnoticed (Proverbs 5:21; 1 Chronicles 28:8,9; Hebrews 4:13). God hears what we say, for no one ever speaks but what it wasn't a thought first (Deuteronomy 5:27,28). If he hears us (which is taking intelligent thought as you listen) you can bet he has a response coming toward us whether now, sometime in this life, or at judgement. God most certainly has thoughts about his creation. He thinks about you all the time (Psalm 139:17). Why don't you talk to him about it sometime? He would love to have a conversation with you, there is so much to learn of his precepts and statutes and he is always willing to listen when you are eager to seek him.

Combating Satan's Thoughts

The battles we face in our mind and heart were originally placed there by the lies of Satan during the time in the garden. His fallen angels and demonic forces are the foes responsible for stealing our peace, our love, our life, and our joy. The law was given to man that he might be reminded of his sin. Through the law, we see, or perceive, good and evil, thereby, recognizing what demonic forces are capable of through sin.

As stated in an earlier chapter, we are reminded through the scriptures, we must learn to do good. How in the world do you learn to do good? Doing good is knowing God, doing God things, living God's way. God is good and by doing good we demonstrate God.

Our minds are at the forefront of this battle. Amos 5:14-15 tells us to seek good and not evil that we may live and to have such a strong force about it as to even hate evil and love good. Hating evil is hating a life that is not dependent upon God, not recognizing Him as Sovereign Creator and not drawing strength from His love. Loving good is akin to loving God, because, once again, God is good (Luke 18:19; Psalm 25:8). You know what good is, it is beautiful, cheerful, pleasant, excellent, lovely, delightful, joyful, precious, the right and it comes from God (HGKSB, Strong's 2896, Hebrew, O.T. *Towb*).

Evil, we have already discussed, is a lack of dependence upon a good God. James 3:14 tells us if we are wise, we will show it by a good conversation, a good behavior, but if we have bitter envy and strife in our hearts we should not be arrogant nor should we take glory for ourselves, thereby, lying against the truth. This kind of wisdom (the lying kind) does not come from above, "but is earthly, natural, demonic" (James 3:15). Satan wants us to stay under the law because the law functions under the flesh. He wants to keep us in the flesh since this is where you have given him authority. Satan is defeated when you become born again by the Spirit. Because Christ overcame the world, and we take part of that overcoming, when we walk in the Spirit partaking of The Shed Blood of Jesus and have the faith of our Father. Our life is now guided by the Spirit, guided by obedience to the Christ and His word, and guided by the love of the Father.

Jealousy, selfish ambition, and strife function in our natural man. As we listen to ideas, comments, opinions, and divisive demonic influence we see how Satan interjects thoughts to get these into our hearts and minds to break us down, to keep us doing evil, to not depend upon God when all of these things are going on around us.[15] Racism, hatred and division accompany this strife which is prelude to every kind of evil thing.

Look at what you believe and why you believe it. You believe what you are comfortable with. You believe what is convenient for you. You believe what allows you to justify yourself. Sin is what allows you to

---

[15] James 3:15, "This wisdom descendeth not from above, but is earthly, sensual, devilish." Earthly is this world system, the place where Satan roams about, where it is his to give to whomever he wishes, (I Peter 5:8; Luke 4:6). Sensual is the natural man, the fallen nature of man, (Jude 1:19). Devilish is demonic influence brought about by Satan and his fallen angels, (Luke 10:18; Isaiah 14:12; Revelation 12:9). Satan, because he was perfect in beauty and wisdom, walking in the Garden of Eden, created for music, anointed to cover, stood upon the mountain of God and walked up and down in the midst of the stones of fire, has been found with iniquity, (Ezekiel 28). Dwelling in such beauty and glory with the God of heaven, when once he looked upon himself, has fallen, now to steal, to kill and to destroy that which God holds dear. He wants in your heart and mind to get you to think thoughts that do not include God. Remember, though, the created is not ever over the creator.

protect your "self" so you don't have to hold yourself accountable to falling short of God's glory. As long as I am doing what I want, doing what I am able to comprehend, I feel like it's okay. We actually take comfort when a leader gets caught doing wrong because it makes it easier to justify our wrongs. We say, "Well, if they can get away with it then I guess I'm not so bad.". Who is lying to whom? Where does that thought come from? Is it God's thought? No, He holds us accountable for every idyll word we speak (Matthew 12:36). Is it our thoughts? It may be if we are drawing attention to ourselves or justifying our actions. Is it Satan's thoughts? Yes, any thought that brings death to our relationship with God is from the demonic realm.

2 Corinthians 10:3-5 tells us that even though we are walking this earth in a fleshly body we do not war after the flesh. The weapons available to us don't come from the flesh realm. But God has given us divinely powerful weapons. The greatest weapon is his Holy Spirit and his gifts. Oh, wait, the greatest weapon is his Word. Oh, wait, it is his mighty angels. Oh, wait, it is his redemption through Jesus. Oh, wait, it is meekness, or prayer, or faith, or doing good, or it is God himself who is love. Our weapons are as infinite as God himself because they come from him.

We achieve success in this warfare by taking captive thoughts, reasonings, and vain imaginations (2 Corinthians 10:5). Bringing into captivity forcefully at spear point we are able to destroy those things that exalt themselves up against the knowledge of God. How? By becoming subject to the commands of God and to his will to save us. In the garden it was his command to not eat from the tree of the knowledge of good and evil. This was the saving grace for Adam and Eve had they remained in obedience to his command they would have been saved from the deception and subsequent fall. Today it is his saving grace through the person Jesus the Christ via his command to love one another. Think about it, if we loved one another the way the Christ loved us and gave himself for us, this world would be a far different world than the one Satan has placed his grasp upon.

You say, "This is just religious jargon, I can say or think what I please, it is my life.". Then you have chosen deception. No life is its own. You didn't just come into being from nowhere. You were conceived by the union of two people. Your life is now connected to those two people. The friends, the enemies, the acquaintances, the ones you love, the ones you hate, the impact you have on them and they have on you is not just happenstance. It has occurred since the creation of man. We are inextricably connected by the Sovereign Creator that is willing to save that which was lost (Matthew 18:11; Luke 19:10).

When you stand on a stage telling everyone, "This is the way you should go," or "This is the way you should believe because this is what I think about it or how I believe," then you have thought yourself to be something you are not. You have placed your life above others and bid them follow you. No, your life is not your own to do as you please with no regard for God, or what others think, or how it affects them.

You say, "Well, isn't that what you are doing here in this book, telling us what we should be thinking about God?". No, I am not telling you what choice to make, that is entirely up to you. I am writing what God is speaking to me. If you choose to think you need to go deeper, checking with God, verifying with scripture what you have read, seeking the word of truth that sets men free, then pursue that path. But, if you think, *This guy is a fruitcake*, then simply put the book down and walk away. As you go, check yourself if you have the courage and ask, "Do the ways I think about a situation, a person, about an idea, about a place, a position, about a moment in time, are they impacted by what comes out of my heart? Do I control my conversations with people by forcing my opinions upon them? Do I take in a thought about an experience that shapes my insecurities? Do I push away people because they appear different to me? Do I do all this to promote and protect myself? What I am saying, or thinking, or doing, does it project humility towards others?"

Go ahead and walk away but don't do it out of fear of what others might think about you, or fear of facing yourself, realizing your insecurities are directly related to your fears. If you do so, your fear is rooted in a false sense of security that says, "You must protect your "self." In order to go forward in life, you must change, when you know him as a God of love, and this is what you think on, this is what you store up in your heart, and this is what you let your life rest on, then you will find your life is not your own (1 Corinthians 6:19,20).

Colossians 3:2,3,10; "Set your mind (center column) on things above, not on things on the earth. For ye are dead, and your life is hid with Christ in God. And have put on the new man, which is renewed in knowledge after the image of him that created him."

2 Corinthians 4:6; "For God, who commanded the light to shine out of darkness, hath shined in our hearts, to give the light of the knowledge of the glory of God in the face of Jesus Christ."

Romans 6:10-11; "For in that he died, he died unto sin once: but in that he liveth, he liveth unto God. Likewise reckon ye also yourselves to be dead indeed unto sin, but alive unto God through Jesus Christ our Lord."

Turn to Philippians 4:7-8 and use this as the litmus test for what you are to be thinking, for the peace you are to experience, for the seeds you want to sow, and for the life you want to give to others. My heart and my mind are kept in peace by God when I am not anxious or careful (fearful of how it affects me) about things in this life.

As we begin the battle for renewing our mind, we must ask ourselves: "What have our thoughts, our mind, our heart been feeding on?" Do we get that happy, cheerful, lovely, peaceful mind from watching the nightly news or planting our face in a phone screen watching violence, pornography, or people making fun of others at that person's expense? When you decide to get with God and renew your mind you can bet Satan will begin to assault your thoughts with what others are saying or incidents at work or home. The battle becomes very real here, but the weapons of our warfare are divinely inspired, they are more than capable of defeating the accuser because the Creator cast him out of heaven, and he is never going to get any better at his attacks.

Back to Philippians 4:8 where we are instructed on what we need to be thinking on, or what we should be giving our attention to. Think on what is true, honest, just, pure, lovely, a good report, virtue, and praise. These are what we need to give thought to. We need to take these thoughts letting them get into our heart, to become who we really are, and who God intended us to be. What is true is solely based on that which God has given us (Proverbs 12:17-19; John 8:32). What is honest is that which does not lie. It speaks truth never promoting itself at the cost of others. What is just is that which provides all with the knowledge that we are to be fair in all we do. There is One who is over us and we shall give account for what we have done (Colossians 4:1; 1 Peter 4:5). What is pure is that which has not been defiled by our greed, our lustful desires, or our self-satisfaction (Philippians 2:15; Hebrews 7:26). What is lovely is that which we can see, we are even able to feel it. It surrounds us when we see people treating others in need with good, how they respond in tears and gratitude. Easily discernable is the opposite: that which is ugly. It also can be seen and felt. When you see harsh words being spoken to purposely ridicule or demoting someone's personality you are witnessing the ugliness of man's fallen nature. When lives are taken needlessly through unmerited acts of violence, this is ugly. It demeans the whole of humanity because it demonstrates how far we have removed ourselves from God's lovely grace (John 13:34-35; Romans 12:9-10). What is of a good report is that which states the reliability of those involved. It brings together truth, honesty, justice and the very character of the individuals or peoples (3 John 1:11,12). What is of virtue is that which promotes excellence in manners and treatment of others, in our deep mercies, our kindnesses, our humbleness of mind, in our meekness and our enduring of life's situations (Colossians 3:12-14). Together these virtues provide power to heal, to overcome and to deliver us from bondages that keep us from freedom (Mark 5:28-34). What is of praise is stepping into the freedom of rising above all that this earthly life throws at us. It brings us out of our lowly self and gives glory to the One who loves us and is willing to deliver us (1 Chronicles 16:23-36). These thoughts are undoubtedly powerful, supernatural weapons in combating Satan's thoughts.

What about the evil that occurs around us every day, what are we supposed to do about confronting this? Romans 12:14-21 gives us good instruction on how we should handle the evil that occurs around us each day. Bless those who curse you – are you able to do that with a heart and mind that harbors hate? Don't be haughty, placing yourself above someone you perceive to be less then you. Are you able to do this with thoughts and a heart that are full of vain pride? When someone does something against you such as saying hurtful words to you, do you lash right back at them calling them everything in the book? Do you have a heart that is willing to trust God to deal with that person? When you strike back you are only doing so to protect yourself and in so doing you immediately remove God from serving justice in the matter and you place yourself into the judgement of God. At this point repent quickly before God and turn the matter back over to Him (Matthew 5:44). Simply put, do not be overcome by evil but overcome evil with good (Romans 12:21).

Get your thoughts on the right things. Make a conscious decision to do Luke 12:34, 'Where your treasure is there will your heart be also." Treasure up that which is good, fill yourself with the love of God, even if you don't understand it all yet. Work out your salvation by applying His word, in faith and love, to all of your thoughts, all of your circumstances and all of the evil that comes against you today.

Herein is the give and take of the weapons of our warfare and of our thoughts and that is this: Our God is, and was, and is to come (Revelation 1:8). It starts with him, it is currently present with him, and it will end with him because God gives. Look at it, He gives us life everlasting because Jesus is life (John 14:6). He gives us peace from himself, not like the temporary and incomplete peace the world gives (John 14:27). His peace gives assurance to our heart and dispels fear. He gives us the Holy Spirit, the Comforter, The Spirit of Truth (John 14:16). He gives us love (John 3:16). He gives us grace (Ephesians 4:7; I Timothy 1:10; Hebrews 2:4). He gives the rain in their season (Leviticus 26:4). He gives us mercy (Matthew 5:7). He gives spiritual gifts to profits us (1 Corinthians 12:7-11). He gives inspiration to write the scriptures that we might profit from doctrine, reprove, rebuke, and exhort ourselves and each other (2 Timothy 3:16). He gives us strength (Psalm 29:11). He gives His angels charge over us to keep us in all our ways (Psalm 91:11). He gives us an inheritance (Acts 20:32). He gives us increase (1 Corinthians 3:7). He gives wisdom (James 1:5). He gives us the keys of the kingdom of heaven (Matthew 16:19). He gives knowledge and skill in all learning and wisdom. (Daniel 1:7). He gives us a new heart (Ezekiel 36:26). He gave us a new commandment, that we love one another (John 13:34). He has given us a spirit of power, a spirit of love, and a spirit of a sound mind (2 Timothy 1:7). He gives us joy to live (Romans 15:13). He gives us His word (John 1:1-4). He gives us snow (Psalm 147:16). He gives seed to the sower to provide bread (2 Corinthians 9:10). He just gives us all things to enjoy (1 Timothy 6:17). As you see all that he gives it is revealed to you who he is, this is revelation of the knowledge of the Lord in his creation, and we are his creation. Everything that exists comes from him the snow and the rain, the gifts of the Holy Spirit, our ability to think and deduce ideas and inventions and it is this perception of a Holy Almighty God that allows us to use this knowledge to overcome in our warfare.

Now these are weapons. This is knowledge of truth. These are not of this earth. They are not of the natural, carnal man. These weapons come down from above. They are pure, peaceable, gentle, reasonable, full of mercy and good fruits, without partiality or hypocrisy, and it is sown in peace by those who make peace (James 3:17-18). This is what God has given mankind to live by so that we may defeat the ways of evil. As you draw closer to God and begin to experience the infinite ways of life that he gives, you begin to understand that those things that frustrated you in the past, or the hurtful words and actions people say and do, or the bad decisions you made that have catapulted you into unfortunate circumstances, all begin to fade into a righteous faith, a holy understanding and trusting of the One who created you.

When our thoughts bring out these weapons from our heart then we know we are dealing with God's thoughts brought forth by the light of His Word. It is up to us to take these, this knowledge of all that he created, all that he gives, as weapons and apply them to our hearts, our thoughts, our actions, our spoken words, and lives. It is this knowing him that changes our lives, our hearts, and our minds. Our selfish thoughts and those thoughts presented by Satan fade in the light of this knowledge, this new creature that is born from above. Weapons are proven in the fire of trial and as we grow in our reliance of the Holy Spirit and his gifts along with the Word of God our trust grows strengthening our faith. Our armor consists of the belt of truth and the breastplate of righteousness along with the shield of faith and the helmet of salvation (Ephesians 6:13-17). These are the necessary components that are required to do warfare. All of this comes together with the sword of the Spirit which is the word of God. It is the word of God spoken through the Spirit of God that ignites the flame that consumes the thoughts of evil produced by our-self or by Satan.

Knowing the Difference

We must recognize the difference between the thoughts that come from our flesh and those injected by Satan. Look at James 3:14 and check yourself, do I have bitter envy or jealousy, and do I have strife? Am I creating a commotion, unsettling the circumstances and people around me? How about Galatians 5:19-21? Are my actions demonstrating immorality or adultery, impurity, or sensuality? How about what I am bowing down to? What demands my pleasure? What do I worship? Do I commit sorcery or witchcraft, which is rebellion to God? How do

I handle my anger, is it uncontrolled? Does my anger control others, causing offense or hurting others, both physically and emotionally? Do I give the right of my mind over to drunkenness? Would I rather dispute someone then to listen with open ears?

These are of your "self", your fleshly carnal nature. You do these because you have allowed your thoughts to fill your heart with these. Satan finds it easy to influence you because you already allow these thoughts to express themselves in your life, your manners, the words that come out of your mouth, the way you treat your circumstances and those who are around you (Genesis 6:5). Your perceptions, coupled with an understanding that has no divine influence are completely clouded by sin, which lies at the door with a desire to have you (Genesis 4:7). Satan uses the mind that weakens itself because it focuses on these evil, carnal, thoughts which allows demonic influence to create in you a stronghold that will keep you in bondage. We do have, through Christ, the right, authority, and mind, to have dominion over sin and the pulling down of strongholds (2 Corinthians 10:4).

Look again at Galatians 5:13-18, we have a liberty given to us when we accept Jesus, being born from above. This liberty is not for our flesh to do as *it pleases* but for our spirit to be alive in Christ. This is why we must renew our mind to bring under subjection our flesh and the thoughts that generate from these jealousies, envies, and strife. The thoughts that lead us to adultery and idolatry did not instantly change you, no, you thought about them over and over, giving them opportunity to take root in your heart. Thoughts that build anger that may eventually take you to the brink of murder have been given your attention for days, weeks or possibly years. When an event or moment explodes in front of you then the anger that has taken root in your heart and mind break forth in uncontrolled rage (read again Genesis 4:3-7 and you will find Cain spent time thinking about himself and his self-pity opened a door that led to an awful outcome that plagues the earth yet today). No, this liberty God has given us is for our spirit, by love, to serve one another.

Satan will initiate the moment that forces us to take a thought, but you ask, "How does he do that?" By lies. Satan is the Father of lies (John 8:44). When Adam and Eve partook of the fruit of the tree of the knowledge of good and evil, at that moment, the failures of sin were conceived and sin, when it is conceived, brings forth death (James 1:15). This made Satan a murderer because his lies brought about the death of the perfect relationship of man and God. He lied and used deception to accomplish this death, this is where fear comes in, think about the last argument you had, were you a little fearful for the attack on your self-justification or perhaps the smackdown of your pride, it is possible when this happens to you in an argument that you can make a choice, let that sin lying at the door come in and overtake you or speak out of the love of God in your heart.

Look at Genesis 3:10. Adam says to God after God called out to him in the garden, "I heard the sound of you in the garden and I was afraid because I was naked, so I hid myself." God knew that man would be faced with a decision to obey or disobey His command to not eat of the fruit of the tree of the knowledge of good and evil. Upon deciding to eat of the fruit man partook of the awareness of the self-sin nature therefore Adam saw he was naked (without the covering of the Holy Spirit) and tried to hide that self-awareness from God. Fear now acts in accordance with death caused by lies and deception as a direct result of the knowledge of sin. Adam experienced something he had never known before. By knowing both good and evil Adam could now see that he was no longer covered by God and he appeared naked without the protection of the Most High. The result of this now is our natural reaction to justify our separation from God and that is to hide ourselves. Without the covering of God in our minds and hearts we allow our thoughts to go uncaptured and we reason them to be okay because it makes us feel alright about ourselves.

Satan is now given permission to use intimidation as a fiery dart to keep us under. Look down through the ages how intimidation has oppressed nations through corrupt governments, how it has oppressed individuals in jobs, marriages, by bullying, at sporting events and on and on. He uses strife or a contentious spirit to bring quarrelling to disrupt peace and bring about all that evil has to offer (James 3:16). He divides us when we refuse to walk in love. He divides us when we become so hard hearted, we will not listen. He divides us when we try to protect ourselves through self-justification. Look how Adam responded to God when God questioned him on who told him he was naked by saying, "The woman you gave me." Wait, she was made from Adam, these two were literally one. Because fear became involved Adam thought it necessary to justify himself at the expense of the woman he loved.

All these tactics Satan uses are overcome by the weapons God gives us. Doing good, peace, hope, faith, taking captive thoughts that come against God, renewing our minds with the Word of God, knowing the promises he has given us. His love, his perfect mature love casts out fear and, really, when you are this deep in his love your love becomes his and he is your love. There is no fear here. This is where trust is at its strongest. This is what dispels doubt. I know whom I have believed (2 Timothy 1:12). This is knowledge of the truth.

As we exercise these weapons God has given us, this knowledge of who He is, we begin to discern quicker those thoughts that come from God, those thoughts that come from ourselves, and those thoughts injected by Satan. You have been living with thoughts from all three arenas all your life, but when you give thought to the arenas of Satan and self, simply repent quickly, forcefully place those thoughts under the blood of Jesus and let His anointing dispose of them, this is the obedience of Christ. Take hold of the promises of the Word of God. Live in love. Live by faith. Begin to take authority by Christ, through God's mercy and grace, casting to the ground void all thoughts that promote evil and yourself and especially those injected by Satan and the demonic realm.

Examples

Examples of some of the people in the Bible may give you the opportunity to see for yourself how regular people did some pretty extraordinary things. How their thoughts along with the process of those thoughts and the resulting outcomes affected their lives and the history of the world.

Elijah

First, let's look at a man named Elijah. This man lived during a time when Israel was divided into two kingdoms - one being Israel and the other Judah. He is also considered one of the mightiest prophets known in the scriptures. He called down fire from heaven, raised the dead back to life and even appeared on the Mount of Transfiguration with Jesus and Moses. Most notably, it is written of him that the Spirit of Elijah will precede the coming of Christ. This is not his spirit but the Spirit of God in him, which quickened his spirit that same Spirit comes to convict of sin, righteousness, and judgement (John 16:8). We are introduced to Elijah for the first time in 1 Kings 17:1 where we find him speaking to the King of Israel.

A little background on the King of Israel will help clarify this coming situation. The King of Israel is Ahab, his father Omri was King before him and while Omri did evil in the sight of the Lord, Ahab did more evil then all who were before him. Ahab married a daughter of the King of the Sidonians (Zidonians) named Jezebel, she got her husband to serve and worship the god Baal, building an altar and places of worship, all of which very much provoked the Lord God of Israel.

One more thing before we get into this story. In the Old Testament, when a prophet spoke the word of God, he nearly always preceded it with a "Thus saith the Lord.", statement which we will touch on in a moment.

We open this story in 1 Kings 17:1 with Elijah speaking directly to the King of Israel, Ahab, and this is what he said, "As the Lord, the God of Israel lives, before whom I stand, there shall not be dew nor rain these years, but according to my word." As previously stated, prophets would first receive instruction from God and as they spoke it they would signify that this is what the Lord said but we don't see, "Thus saith the Lord." here. Elijah made a statement, born out of the Spirit, that demonstrated the confidence that was in his heart built on knowing the will of God and that God would back him up.

Let's break this statement down, first, "As the Lord, the God of Israel lives,", perfectly establishes with Ahab that Israel has a God and he lives. He is not made by human hands. Secondly, "before whom I stand," commands that Elijah is in the presence of the Lord. Thirdly, "there shall be neither dew nor rain these years, except by my word.", demonstrates the courage and confidence Elijah has in the full assurance that God will perform the actions spoken by the prophet. Lastly, he puts exactness to what he speaks, no dew, no rain and it is going to be for this long. This is undoubtedly a very bold and strong statement to this King who knows the history of Israel and knows the Lord God is the great, "I Am," but chooses to defy the God of Israel in all that he does as King.

Now, in verse 2, the word of the Lord comes to Elijah to instruct him for his safety and protection.[16] God says, "Get out of here and go to

---

[16] God has, from the beginning of creation, provided us with His word to provide safety, protection and provision for us to live by. From Genesis 2:16,17 to Deuteronomy 8:1-10, to Jesus using this very word to contend with Satan in Matthew 4:4. Man does not live by bread alone, it simply is not the lusts of our appetites that we think sustains us, it is the Word God speaks to create, to form life, love and faith. He sent His word for our healing of the struggles of life and hardships that break and humble us which also prove His Word in our hearts. Will we give Him glory for His providence in our lives despite the difficulties and decisions we encounter or will we harden our hearts turning from the Holy One that loves us as He disciplines us out of this love? The result of humbling and learning the value of His word is that we may know what is in our hearts. As we walk in His word and His ways, fearing Him as a consuming fire, dividing soul and spirit, He will bring us into a good land which should lead us to one response and that is to, "…bless the LORD thy God for the good land which he hath given thee.", (Deuteronomy 8:10).

71

this brook so you will have water to drink and bathe with and I will have the birds bring you your food (1 Kings 17:2 paraphrased). Elijah does this and after a period of time, because there is no rain, God continues His instruction to move on since the brook has dried up. He says go to Zarephath and meet this widow woman, whom I have commanded to provide for you. So, off Elijah goes to meet the widow woman. Do to the drought she only has enough food to make the last meal for her son and herself. Well, what flour and oil she had, Elijah told her to go ahead and make a meal for him first.[17] If this is your last meal and someone tells you to make it for them, I'm not sure this is what you want to hear let alone comply with. But Elijah in verse 13 says, "Do not fear." Remember, fear is a byproduct of lies and deceit. The lie here would be, did God really command you to give your last meal to this man, surely you will starve your son and yourself? This is a good place for doubt to step in. Now he says in verse 14, "Thus saith the Lord," the bowl of flour will not run out and the jar of oil will not go empty until the Lord sends the rain on the earth thus giving confidence to the widow woman that the matter is of the Lord and they are in His hands (1 Kings 17:3-4 paraphrased).

See what is happening here, Elijah is telling her, God is responsible to carry out what he had spoken to King Ahab and to what God had commanded her in providing for Elijah. We must also note here that once the rain came the bowl of meal and jar of oil would be running out. However, the bowl and jar had to be big enough to sustain the widow and her son until the crops were sown, cultivated, and harvested. You never get a harvest from the first rain this will come in the latter rain. [18]

---

[17] God had commanded the widow woman to provide for Elijah, when he shows up, she most certainly wanted to be sure this was the guy God had commanded her about. She follows his instruction at the peril of not providing her son and herself with their last meal facing starvation. Her obedience to the prophet's instructions were also obedience to what God had commanded her. The barrel of meal and cruse of oil did not fail during this obedience. God brings provision when we do His word.

[18] God brings the rain in his season to produce the fruit of the ground. Harvest comes

Sometime after all this the widow woman's son becomes severely sick and stops breathing. The widow looks at Elijah and says, "what are you doing here showing me my sin and to put my son to death?" Elijah takes the boy and calls on God when God hears Elijah He revives the boy by restoring his soul back into him. After all this the woman gets understanding and confirmation that Elijah is a man of God, the one God commanded her to provide for and that the word of the Lord that comes from his mouth is truth. In other words, what is in the heart of Elijah, what he thinks, what comes out in his spoken words are as though they are God's words Himself.

To me chapter 18:1 is quite possibly the greatest verse in this story. The time had come for God to accomplish what Elijah originally spoke to King Ahab. Once again, the confidence, the knowing Elijah had about who his God is, produces boldness. God gives instruction to Elijah, "Go show yourself to Ahab, and *I will send rain.*" Elijah spoke what was in his heart because it aligned with God's heart. God supported the courage of Elijah by taking responsibility to produce the rain. Elijah, as a man, can't make it rain that is God's doing and this is the confidence Elijah had knowing God would perform it. God is willing and faithful to perform His word when you speak what is in His heart. He does what He says (Isaiah 55:10,11).

This is a great verse because it proves he is with us and he is responsible and faithful to perform it. When we have thoughts that are filling our heart with the courage of the Word of God, the knowing and trusting that he is with us, then we are able to encourage our self. We are able to take the weapons of our warfare, the peace, the Spirit of grace, the Spirit of Truth, hope, faith and the power of love and forgiveness, doing good and on and on, becoming able to apply these weapons against the evil that is set in this world today.

---

after the early rains for growing. When the Spirit of God rains truth upon you during the Spring and warmth of the Summer learn to abide in Him, resting on the word and grow in faith. The Widow woman came to know that the Word of God in Elijah was true by seeing the faithfulness of God being fulfilled before her very eyes. (James 5:7-8; Joel 2:23)

Ahab finally comes to meet Elijah and the first thing out of his mouth is, "Are you the one who troubles Israel?" (1 King 18:17 paraphrased). This is often the case, when individuals or groups who are following their agenda and it is contrary to God, they like to turn the table projecting their wickedness on the one who is doing right. Once again, Ahab, asking this question, knew the history of Israel, he knew that Baal was not the true God but chose to serve him anyway. Because he is in the wrong, he has to protect himself by projecting the fault back on to Elijah. But Elijah sets the record straight in verse 18 and held nothing back in doing so, "I have not troubled Israel but you *and* your father's because *you* have forsaken the commandments of the Lord *and* you have followed Baal." (1 Kings 18:18 paraphrased). Elijah turns the table right back around and pinpoints the real troubler of Israel because they had removed themselves from the protection and provision of the word of God. Kings are generally the ones commanding people what to do but not here, Elijah tells Ahab, "NOW gather all Israel to me at Mount Carmel" (1 Kings 18:19 paraphrased). When you are in the same heart as the Lord it is amazing the authority you will have. Ahab knew that Elijah spoke truth since what he had spoken three and a half years earlier concerning the rain had come to pass.

The Proposition to Make a Decision

Everyone has gathered there, Elijah, King Ahab, all of Israel, the prophets of Baal and Asherah, everyone except for Queen Jezebel has gathered on Mount Carmel. Before all who are present Elijah asks a very poignant question, "How long halt ye between two opinions?" (1 Kings 18:21). To "halt" is a word used to describe a limp or to pass over or to dance around making a decision. You have a mind knowing the truth yet is still seeking self-satisfaction. Thoughts go nowhere when they are not decided upon. They will breed complacency, inactivity, a lack of passion and ultimately, they produce waste.

When you're doing wrong and you are confronted with the one question that cuts right to the heart of the situation, your first reaction is usually silence while your mind is deciding to either justify itself or swallow your pride and listen to what is being pinpointed. When Elijah posed the question that exposed their rebellion against God all Israel did not say a word. Elijah than makes a proposition that will force Israel to make a decision. The 450 prophets of Baal were to pick out an ox, prepare it for a sacrifice, set it upon a pile of wood and get ready to call upon their god to consume the sacrifice with fire. Elijah would do the same with his oxen. Neither side was to kindle the fire for the sacrifice.

Here comes the call to make a decision. Baal prophets were to call on the name of their god and Elijah would call on the name of Yahweh and the god who answers by fire, he is God. So, if we do this, you will have to make a decision Israel. The prophets of Baal and the people of Israel all knew about the God of Israel, so, both groups of people had to have their minds engaged in a thought process concerning this proposal. The people of Israel may have been thinking, *"We have heard all these stories about God, how he delivered our people out of Egypt, so, yeah, it might be good for us to see the power of God in our day and time."* When you think this way, know this; if you so strongly desire to see the power of God, then you best be prepared to deal with the consequences of the choice you will be faced with. The Baal prophets may have thought, *"I have given myself to the god Baal, this is what I believe, this will be a great opportunity for the people to see that what I believe is right."* Everyone replied to Elijah, "That's a good idea, those are good words." (1 Kings 18:24).

It is important to note here that neither the prophets of Baal nor the Israelite people were acting in faith. Faith doesn't compel us to act complacent about anything. Faith only functions in truth, regardless of what you allow yourself to be deceived to believe. Remember, Elijah was one man standing against thousands, but he had faith, he knew the outcome.

The prophets of Baal set themselves to the task, preparing the ox for sacrifice and placing it upon the pile of wood, then they began to call on the name of their god Baal. Uh, you could hear the crickets chirping long about now. They tried leaping and dancing, even jumping upon the altar. This went on all morning until noontime.

Imagine, if you will, all the people sitting on Mount Carmel watching this production the entire morning waiting to see what might happen. By this time Elijah gives them a little encouragement, "Maybe you need to yell a little louder, or maybe he went somewhere, or he is taking a nap and you need to wake him up." (1 Kings 18:27). So they yelled louder and really wanted to amp things up and started to cut themselves. You have a bunch of crazed people yelling, jumping all over the place, cutting themselves with blood flying everywhere. What a scene unfolding in front of the Israelite people. This went on clear through the afternoon, can you imagine what foolishness this looked like? No matter how loud they called, how high they leaped, how much blood they shed, no one answered, no voice was heard, no one even gave them attention (1 Kings 18:29). This had to be an incredibly sad sight to see.

Onto the stage steps Elijah and he said to all the people, "Come near to me." Mount Carmel already had an altar upon it that the Israelites had previously worshipped at sacrificing to God on it. Elijah repaired the altar that had been torn down. This says it all as concerning Israel and their relationship with Jehovah. They didn't stand with God and by tearing down His altar, proved their rebellion towards Him. They did not stand with God they limped and danced around in their attitudes toward Baal and towards the God of Israel. Are we not the same, hearing about God, but living as though it is not necessary to live for Him? Rather, we say we believe in a higher power, yet we live in this world to please ourselves. How long halt ye between two opinions?

Elijah used twelve stones to rebuild the altar representing the twelve sons of Jacob who become the nation of Israel. Now he did something the prophets of Baal didn't do, he added water. Four pitchers, or large jars, filled with water poured out on the altar of stones, the oxen sacrifice, the wood, and the trenches dug around the altar. Not once but three times (4 x 3=12) one jar of water for each of the twelve tribes of Israel, demonstrating that, right now, right here, there would be cleansing and baptism for the twelve tribes of Israel if they so choose. He alone can cleanse our minds, heal our thoughts, and forgive us for our rebellion. How the Lord uses symbolism can send a powerful message.

The altar was soaked, the trenches that were dug around the altar were filled, the entire altar was baptized under water. Elijah calls on God saying, "I have done all this at your word." God had, by his word, given Elijah what to do and in obedience and faith he did what he was told. What Elijah says next we should consider as a "verily, verily" moment. In other words, it is very important so pay attention. "Hear me that this people may know that you are the Lord God and that you turned their heart back again." (1 Kings 18:37). First, that the people may know. This means their thoughts acknowledge he is *the Lord God*. Secondly, that it is not Elijah that performed this: He just did what he was told. Thirdly, it is the Most High God himself that turns hearts back to him.

Fire fell! King Ahab and all the people of Israel standing on this mountain, all the prophets of Baal who had literally worn themselves out jumping around all day long, bleeding everywhere, all watching this amazing scene of fire so intense fall from heaven that it consumed the sacrifice of the ox, the wood, the stones, the dust and even the water. Nothing was left. The immediate reaction of anyone watching this unfold before their very eyes would be the same as Israel did here. They fell on their faces.

What comes out of their mouth has always caused me to wonder about the sincerity of the Israelites. They said, "The Lord, He is God." They didn't say, "The Lord, He is *our* God.", or "The Lord, He is *The* God.", no, it just seems they acknowledge He won that fight. It wasn't long afterwards that Israel was back to doing what they had been doing before this event, not fearing the LORD of Hosts, not trusting him for deliverance, and still being caught up in having a divided mind.

The prophets of Baal are rounded up and destroyed. Rebellion only has two paths to follow, one is repentance and the other is destruction. People who rebel against the truth of the word of God and do not repent, but continue in their rebellion, will at the appointed time face destruction.

After the destruction of the Baal prophets Elijah goes back to the top of Mount Carmel, falls down with his face between his knees and has his servant go look toward the sea. The servant says, "I don't see anything." Seven times this is done, and the servant says on the seventh time, "Behold a cloud as small as a man's hand is coming up out of the sea." (1 Kings18:43-44). This has been a long day with a whole lot of action and drama going on. Jumping, screaming, bleeding, a day full of symbolism with fire falling from heaven, all the prophets of Baal being destroyed, thunder clouds coming on the horizon after over three years of drought, yes this was a jammed packed day even by today's standards. But it is not over, Elijah sends Ahab back to Jezreel to get ready to celebrate the rain. After this long full day, Elijah, being powered by the word God had given him this day and the consuming fire of the Holy Spirit, girded up his loins and literally ran ahead of King Ahab to the entrance of Jezreel.

Ahab, when he gets to Jezreel, goes to his wife, Jezebel, describing what had just transpired today on Mount Carmel - how Elijah watched the prophets of Baal fail to get a response from their god, How he called down fire from heaven consuming the sacrifice, and how he rounded up the prophets of Baal killing them while running ahead of Ahab to Jezreel (1 Kings 18:46; 19:1). Jezebel is not Jewish. She has never served the God of Israel. The prophets of Baal used to sit at her table. This was a powerful intrusion upon her belief and way of life. We must ask ourselves when something comes along that challenges, or even threatens to destroy our belief system, or our way of life, how do we respond? Know this. If God is challenging you, the destruction you face will be the death of self, but the new life of the Spirit equipped with grace, mercy, and love will be there to fill you. If you are in rebellion, and you are not aware that you are rebellious, trust assured God will provide an awakening which may not always be pleasant for sure.

Look at Jezebel's response. How it is directly proportioned to protecting herself and motivated by fear. Ask yourself. Who did the prophets of Baal receive their instruction from? We already know there was no voice, no answer and no one even regarded these prophets. In other words, no Baal. These prophets never heard from Baal they heard from Jezebel. She instructed them. She held sway over them. She controlled them. She was the one under demonic influence and it deceived the weak minds of the prophets of Baal. Even Elijah saw the effort put forth by the prophets of Baal with no results, no one answered them but when Jezebel sends her message to Elijah, everything changed.

Pay attention to the fine details, Ahab rode to Jezreel where Jezebel was. Elijah outran Ahab to the entrance of Jezreel, so, both Elijah and Jezebel were in the same area. You must realize when you encounter the spirit of Jezebel, she is very threatening and controlling, but she avoids confrontation, knowing she may not be able to defend or protect herself. She draws her strength from the fear that drives her. God is not afraid. He assures us not to be afraid, (Isaiah 41:10).

Jezebel could have gathered her forces and straightway confronted Elijah instead she sends a messenger telling Elijah that by this time tomorrow she plans on making his life like the life of one of her prophets that he killed. The word for "life" used here gives us the term used for an animal's life, for our minds, our desires, it is essentially our soulish realm. This, after all, is what Satan is after - our souls. He cannot have our spirit unless he has our soul. Ah, but Elijah, obviously being wearied from this challenging day, upon hearing the message received from Jezebel, was sorely affected by it. Some translations interpret it to read, "He was afraid", the KJV reads, "And when he saw", this is the same Hebrew word we discussed earlier that occurred in Genesis at creation when the woman saw the fruit. Here, Elijah saw the message, literally, looked at, regarded it, felt it, experienced it by taking thought that his soul was endangered. He made a mental perception that he may be in trouble. James 5:17 tells us Elijah was a man subject to like passions or feelings so, he ran. He did not confront. He ran. Don't become judgmental here because we are no different. Look at the confrontations in our lives that we run from. Difficulties in our marriages. We don't confront them in love and forgiveness. A friend may be doing something that bothers us or hurts our feelings, and we don't confront it in prayer and trust. Someone may be intimidating, or bullying us, and we run from it. We become fearful. We begin to fill our thoughts with what that other person is saying. Instead, we should be using our weapons of warfare, by finding our courage and our self-esteem from the word of God, the love of God and the grace of God. Hebrews 4:12 reveals to us the power of his Word. It is living. It is sharp and piercing. It is able to divide our soulish realm from that, which moves in the spirit realm, and it is able to discern, or judge our thoughts and the very things that have filled our heart.

We need to rely on the word of God. Elijah had been relying on what God had said for over three years since the time he first addressed King Ahab. But he gets to this point, and possibly, in his weariness, he thinks on what Jezebel said letting those thoughts overtake the words God had spoken to him.

What happens to us when we reach this point of weariness? When we have been zealous for something, reaching ever so close to the end but not yet getting there. How do we feel about ourselves? Where do we go from here? Elijah ran to the desert continuing on another day's travel into the wilderness.[19] All the events that occurred on Mount

---

[19] The desert, the dry places in our lives are where we should be thirsty. This is where we need to drink of the living waters that flow from the person of the Holy Spirit. The wilderness is a place where it is easy to end up wandering around with no destination, lost if you will in the terrain of hardships and difficulties. This is where the Word of Life sustains us, giving us direction and sustenance - the Bread of Life.

Carmel that day and yet he doesn't stop for another day. At this point he has reached the end of his physical endurance and is worn down mentally. Words of faith have a hard time coming out of our mouths when we reach this point. Elijah spoke about himself at this moment. He said, "That is enough." How many times have we said, "I can't do this anymore I've had enough?" Then he compares himself to someone else, "I am not better than my fathers" (1 Kings 19:4). Is this not one of the most common things we do when we have encountered difficulties and weariness? We compare ourselves to our parents, our sisters, our brothers, a competitor, a friend - so many to compare ourselves to. We usually do a comparison with someone we believe is better than us. [20]This comes simply from the weakness of our flesh. Everything he said here came from the what he had been thinking about since Jezebel's messenger had given him this threat upon his life. When once you take a thought and begin to dwell on it, it will lead to other thoughts that grow and overtake the righteousness, the peace, the faith that is ours as sons and daughters of God.

My Grandmother used to have the most beautiful flower garden which she tended diligently, removing those unwanted weeds. However, in her later years, she was unable to tend the garden the way she used to, and those weeds came in and over time obliterated the beauty of those flowers. There were still flowers blooming but they didn't take center stage any longer. Well, don't let weariness cause you to stumble, take captive those thoughts, they are just like weeds always trying to come in and choke out the beauty. There is beauty in His word, a strength, a power and authority, blessing, honor, and life.

---

[20] Comparison may or can be a demonic tool Satan uses to keep our thoughts in the flesh since this is where he has the authority. We are created by God Himself in the image of the Father, the Son, and the Holy Spirit. We are formed in our Mother's womb by the amazing process of conception and He guides the development of the cells. Do not allow your insecurities to dictate your thoughts about how or who you are. Force the living word of God into your heart and know you are fearfully and wonderfully made (Psalm 139:14).

Elijah now moved to the second phase of attacks on his thoughts which is rehearsing his side of the story. God always presents a question to us that will cut straight through the circumstances to the one thing that needs to be weeded out of our heart and mind. God says to Elijah, "What are you doing here?" What was Elijah doing there? Why had he run from Jezebel? What was in him that caused him to fear? Elijah's answer is this, "I have been very jealous, or zealous for you God, the Lord of hosts. Because the children of Israel have forsaken your covenant, they have torn down the altars to you and they have slain your prophets with the sword. I am the only one left and they seek my life, they want to kill me." (1 Kings 19:10 paraphrased).

He wasn't there because he had been zealous for God he had just challenged Israel about their indecisiveness. He wasn't there because the children of Israel had forsaken the covenant with God or because they had torn down the altars, remember he rebuilt the altar. No, he was there because he feared for his life[21]. Jezebel's threat had pushed hard into his thoughts and he left off of the powerful word of God. The irony of this for Elijah is found in 2 Kings chapter 2, Elijah does not die, he is taken up. God took Elijah by a whirlwind in a chariot of fire, he didn't see death. What an exit!

Yes, Jezebel is a formidable foe. She intimidates through fear. She controls by being domineering. She spreads rebellion to God, which is witchcraft. She oppresses freedom, and she threatens our lives. But it is all empty. It is hollow. Her authority is only in the flesh. She has no power in the spirit. When we take captive those thoughts Jezebel is using to strike fear into us, and we bring them into the obedience of

---

[21] Elijah's job was to confront the rebellion of the King and the people of Israel, to destroy the false prophets and bring an end to the intimidation, control and fear of Jezebel. God asked him, "What are you doing here?" He should have been back finishing the job God had anointed him for. He had already exposed the compromising, rebellious spirit, he had already repaired the altar for worship to God and he had already destroyed the false prophets. What he didn't finish was confronting Jezebel and her controlling, intimidating spirit. No, he wasn't at Mount Horeb for those things, he was there because he feared for his life. Fear is crippling. Faith that works by love is liberating.

Christ, we are choosing who we are listening to. The word obedience is essentially to listen, to harken to something. It is a willing subjection to that, which is right (HGKSB, Strong's 5218 N.T. *Hupakoe*). Who are you listening to? The powerful living word of God or the fear and intimidation of Jezebel?

Are we taking captive the thoughts that bring fear and death and are we taking the living word of truth and giving ourselves over to it? Look at your life right now. Are you being controlled and intimidated? Are you in a state of compromise, which is rebellion to God? Is your freedom being oppressed? When you lose your right to choose between life and death you have fallen in your thoughts to the Jezebel spirit. Remember, the weapons of our warfare are not of the flesh. They are divinely powerful. They come from above, from our Father in heaven, from the Spirit of truth and comfort. They come from Jesus the Living Word, and they mightily overcome the ways of the flesh.

Take the grace Jesus gives to find your strength. Take the divine love to destroy fear and death. Take the inspired word of promise to establish your hope. These weapons overcome the world because Jesus overcame the world for us.

The rest of this story shows us how God handled this situation for the anointing that was on Elijah. Elijah looked at the strong wind and God wasn't there. Elijah looked at the earthquake that shook the earth and God wasn't there. Elijah looked at the fire that consumes everything, and he wasn't there. But he found him in "a delicate whispering as of the breeze among the leaves" (1 Kings 19:12 center column). Do yourself a favor, when God asks you, "What are you doing here?" don't rehearse your side of the story. Speaking the problem and continually rehearsing it only removes you farther from his presence. We all may tend to look for this almighty, powerful God in the actions of a powerful wind, or an earth shaking event, or a consuming fire, but if we repent quickly and shut up, we just might hear this delicate whispering, this rustling of the leaves, this still small voice of God that is all and everything we need.

God points out to Elijah that at no point was he alone, seven thousand Israelites had not bowed to Baal or kissed him thereby swearing allegiance to him. You are never alone when God is on your side. God also instructs Elijah to anoint a King over Syria and anoint a King over Israel and to anoint a prophet to take his place.

The beauty of this is even though Elijah stumbled, God spoke with him. The fearfulness of this is God set in motion the plan to finish the job by passing the anointing to others to overtake the rebellious leaders, destroy Jezebel and set the time for Elijah to be taken up. God loves us but will always perform His word with, or without you. Take captive your thoughts to the obedience of Christ, the willingness to humble yourself and do His word.

We have, through this story of Elijah, seen the power of God through the word, the thoughts, and intents of the heart, the repercussions of yielding to fear and the strength, courage, and authority applied by faith, knowing he is with us. Now let's look at another example. Please turn to the Book of Nehemiah, and we shall see what covenant and inheritance can accomplish in the weapons of our warfare by taking captive our thoughts to the obedience of Christ.

Nehemiah

Nehemiah was living during the captivity of Israel that began during the Babylonian Empire and continuing into the Persian Empire. It is, according to some historians, quite possible that Esther may have been queen of the Persian Empire during this time. This, however, is not the reason we are here taking a look at Nehemiah, that is a discussion for historians. Suffice it to know that God had placed people in positions that would interact in each other's lives to accomplish his word. The reason we are here is to witness how this man came against enemies who used fear, intimidation, deceit, and rumors in an effort to thwart the work of God amongst the Jews.

Remember the example of Elijah, how he was part of one of the great events in the Bible, yet he succumbed to fear and intimidation. Now look at Nehemiah his job was to drink the wine before the King would drink to see if it were poisoned. What prepared him to have this responsibility before the most powerful person of the Empire? Elijah after being threatened by Jezebel became concerned about himself and the welfare of his life. Nehemiah could not be concerned about himself, his life, in order to be trusted at such a high level. There was no self-gratification. How often do we read the word of God, pray for people, talk to others about Jesus but still get caught in thoughts of fear or thoughts that steal our peace or our joy? How many times have we had big accomplishments at work or sports or in ministry or simply our personal life, only to be bombarded with thoughts of condemnation, or inadequacies, or even failure that are hell bent on stealing our peace, or that ruin an enjoyable moment, or even try to destroy the big accomplishment that was achieved? If self-satisfaction becomes the driving force in our thoughts it most certainly will cloud our thoughts, how we perceive something and our decision making.

Nehemiah was in a conversation with his brethren listening to the account being told him concerning the state of affairs of the Jewish people which remained in Israel and the condition of the city of Jerusalem. They spoke to him of the great affliction and reproach of the people as well as the walls having been torn down with the gates being burned with fire. Upon hearing this news, he sat down and wept and mourned and began to fast and pray for a period of time. This news struck deep into his heart igniting this powerful passion. A passion which has the ability to cause you to move, to go beyond yourself, for you cannot continue on as you were any longer. He prayed for his people. He confessed his sin, his family's sin, and the sin of his people. He asks God to remember what he had spoken to Moses that if his people will turn to God and keep his commandments that God would be responsible for bringing the people back to the place he had chosen to set his name. He reminded God that this people now belonged to

God himself because they were redeemed by great power and a strong hand. He closed the first chapter by asking God, for those who feared the name of God, to prosper him and grant him mercy in this endeavor that was about to unfold before him.[22]

We asked what had prepared Nehemiah for what he was going to be thrust into, and we find the answer here in chapter 1. Nehemiah had learned, through captivity and holding the position of cup bearer to the King, to not live for himself. To not be concerned about what might benefit him. To not even take thought how this is not the way he thought his life would be. He had given himself to God and would turn to God alone for the answers to the circumstances that engulfed his life. You should be aware at this point, even though you may read this and think, *That's it, I can't do this. I am not ready to give myself up. I don't even know how or what I should be giving up.* "You are not above my love" says the Lord. He is! He is not willing that any should perish. You may end up taking years to go through this process, or you may, in a moment, catch this revelation. Don't give thoughts of unbelief, doubt, insecurity, distrust, and discouragement the opportunity to take you captive. When you first have one of those thoughts, immediately take it captive. Do not be concerned about yourself but say out loud, "I have the mind of Christ" (1 Corinthians 2:16).

Look at the example of Nehemiah - how he was struck deep in his heart about the people of Israel and their condition. How he fasted and prayed, confessing the sin of his people to the Most High God. Now look at how God had set this all-in motion to accomplish His word. Nehemiah must have been a very settled person to always stand before the King testing his drink never having had a sad countenance. How

---

[22] Two different men living during the captivity of Israel and both had lived in the Palace of Shushan, one was Daniel and the other was Nehemiah. Both men fasted and prayed, both sought the Lord in repentance. The similarities in how they confessed to the God of Israel the rebellion and breaking of Moses covenant is striking. Both ask God to remember the covenant and mercy and redemption God promised Israel. Both were willing to lay aside their lives for the fulfilling of God's word. Both sought the inheritance given through the covenant promise of God. Read Nehemiah chapter 1 and Daniel Chapter 9.

often does something happen to us and the sadness shows in our face? Well, the King noticed and knew it must be nothing less than sorrow of heart.

Here is a defining moment in this story. Nehemiah was, "very sore afraid." You know that King Artaxerxes was the ruler of the Persian Empire, one of the great empires of history and, as ruler, he held the life-or-death sentence of all within the empire. Remember Elijah was faced with the same fear of life, but the next thought that each man took is the difference in the results of their stories. When asked by the King what was troubling him Nehemiah stated his grievance, very short, to the point and with specifics. When the King asked, "What would you request?" We know fear was definitely present, but despite that fear, what was truly deep in his heart broke forth. The passion in his heart was no doubt unleashed in his response – the very thoughts that he had been praying and fasting over for a period of time came out in word and passion.

When you have something stored up in your heart that has captured your thoughts over and over you need to begin to measure it against the Word of God. Be careful not to be deceived by the deceitfulness of sin for when it is measured against the truth it may be very difficult to come to terms with it. Nehemiah's trust in God and his lack of concern for self; kept the fear in check.

Elijah poured out his grievance to God while Nehemiah poured out his grievance to the King with the defining moment for Nehemiah being what he did after the King asked him what he wanted to do. "So, I prayed to the God of heaven." During the intensity of the moment he prayed to God. Elijah ran. Nehemiah prayed. One man is not better or worse than the other, this is just how their thoughts evoked their response. The scriptures don't tell us what he prayed but, in this moment, Nehemiah was faced with taking a thought. He could have feared and doubted and began to take thoughts that could have paralyzed him, which would have destroyed his passion. Instead, he chose to pray to

God, thereby, solidifying the path his thoughts would take. The path to trust God with the answer *and* the outcome. He used the weapons of the "word that thou commanded thy servant Moses" (Nehemiah 1:8); and repentance, "I and my father's house have sinned" (Nehemiah 1:6); and promise, "I will gather you from the most remote part of the heavens" (Nehemiah 1:9); and mercy from God passed down through the King, "grant him mercy in the sight of this man." (Nehemiah 1:11).

Do not think because you don't understand the situation or circumstance you are in, that this God thing doesn't work. What have your thoughts been on for the last month, the last year, ten years, fifty years? What is in your heart? Are you taking God's word and promises – his covenant – pushing those thoughts into your inner most man? When trouble comes (and it will), these God thoughts are what come out of you, or are you taking that fear and doubt, deception and self-preservation thoughts and thinking on these things?

Now that Nehemiah was knee deep in this moment with the king, praying to God, standing on the covenant and promises of God, solidifying the path his thoughts would follow he became very emboldened. He laid out exactly what his plan was, "I want to go back to my hometown, the one captured to reinforce the wall, build the gates and doors, and strengthen my people." That's bold! But he goes on, "You are going to give me a letter stating your approval as well as giving me timbers from your forests to build those gates." (Nehemiah 2:5-8). I have obviously paraphrased this in a manner to emphasize the strength and courage that produce boldness. How it is derived from the covenant promise of life and inheritance of a child of God that knows the God of Covenant and believes, by faith, that God is faithful and will never forsake us. The last part of verse 8 in chapter 2 sums it up for the believer, "… And the King granted me, according to the good hand of my God upon me." God was working and Nehemiah acknowledged it.

Enter the Enemy

Nehemiah introduces us to three men: one was a Horonite (possibly a Moabite), one was an Ammonite and the third was an Arabian. Sanbalat, Tobiah and Gesham. These are the three men singled out from all the people of the lands round about Jerusalem that spoke out against the Jews. As the story of Nehemiah unfolds, we see these men raise conflict, use fear and intimidation, spread rumors and deceit in an effort to dissuade the Jews from accomplishing the work God had set them at task to perform.

Sandbalat seems to be the main character of the three men mentioned, yet it is plain to see the three were all affected the same way at the news of the Jewish people. I guess a good question to ask at this juncture of the story would be what is wrong with the Jews rebuilding and establishing themselves again? Why do the Moabites, the Ammonites and the Arabians not want the Jews to succeed?[23] These people recalled the times Israel ruled and how often the God of Israel prevailed over them in ways their gods could not overcome. They knew a strong Israel would cause them to be put under a Covenant God, possibly facing destruction. So short of repenting and deciding to follow the one true God, they cling to their unbelief and rejection. When Nehemiah arrives in Jerusalem with the approval of the King, an escort of Captains of the army and horsemen along with timbers for building, obviously, this news did not set well with these three men. There is a progression these three men follow during this story starting with when

---

[23] Psalm 83 gives a brief rundown of these same kind of people. Verse 3 tells us they have, "taken crafty counsel", against the people of Israel, to cut them off from being a nation and not even be remembered anymore. The Psalmist responds in verse 17 that God confound them, trouble them and put them to shame, for this outcome found in verse 18, that men may know, whose name alone is Jehovah, is the Most High over all the earth. David was the second King of Israel, Nehemiah was toward the latter end of the captivity, the enemies against God (those who chose to not follow Him, obey Him and love Him) will always be against those chosen by God (those who have decided to follow the One who redeemed them from the curse). Even today this is playing out right before our very eyes. Do not think it a strange thing when you see this occurring. Instead do what Nehemiah did - pray, expect Him to perform His covenant and live like you have an inheritance through Christ.

they first knew a man was come to seek the welfare of the children of Israel to the final completion of building the wall (Nehemiah 2:10).

When they heard of it, they grieved exceedingly, (2:10). They laughed the Jews to scorn and despised them interjecting an untruth that sounded logical (2:19). Upon hearing the Jews were progressing and building, they took great indignation and began to mock the Jews (4:1). As they heard the walls were built up, they became very angry (4:17). Hearing there was no breach left in the wall; they resorted to deceitful diplomacy (6:2). A lie was devised, and they began to set forth a rumor of falsehood, (6:5-6). Finally, they hired a person who, on the outside, looked good with good intentions but tried to entrap Nehemiah to do wrong, (Nehemiah 6:10-13).

Do you recognize any of these attempts whether in your personal life, or things you see in public at varying levels? Look at them again, grieved exceedingly, having someone that is just disturbed by you a lot. Someone who laughs or ridicules you then speaks things against you that are untrue. How about someone who gets very heated with you and then makes fun of you? What about someone who is just plain angry with what you are doing? Have you ever had anyone who seems to be diplomatic yet in a very deceitful way? Anyone you know that spreads rumors about you to tear down your character? Possibly you have encountered someone who had been put up to lying to you by someone else just to ruin you. These are all familiar to us in varying forms and at different times of our lives, yet we have all encountered some of these in our lives, or the lives of someone we know.

Recognize these as attempts of the enemy to derail us. If you do not know Jesus as your Savior you will respond to these attacks by offense, emotional upheaval, opinions, and judgements and quite possibly reacting back to that person with the with same ill they perpetrated on you. If you do have Jesus as your Savior and you respond the same way than you better repent and ask God to get your mind and heart right.

How much time in our life have we wasted letting our thoughts get wrapped up in these shallow attacks?

Let's check out how Nehemiah responded to these attacks. When he came into town, he did not tell anyone what God had put in his heart to do. After three days he gets up at night, takes a few men with him and does an inspection tour to get an idea of what the conditions were firsthand. With a clear knowledge of the conditions of the city he presents his case to the people. These same people were not taken away into the captivity they were left behind as a remnant. These same people had little to no resources to accomplish much of anything they were just trying to survive. These same people were under the intimidation of the Moabites, Ammonites and Arabians unable to give any thought to rebuilding the wall. Nehemiah then declares the bad state of the city and how God has shown him favor and inspiration and how the King has given his approval. He does so in such a passionate way it stirs the people and they respond, "Let us rise up and build." (Nehemiah 2:17-18). These same people living under duress, struggling to survive with truly little hope now see an opportunity to change. They took this encouragement, which strengthened their hands, knowing this would be a good work. They realized they had authority now and that God was demonstrating His covenant promise.

Enter the enemy, the three guys who did not want to see Israel succeed. They laughed and said, "What are you doing? What a pathetic effort, you've got nothing." (paraphrased Nehemiah 2:19). This is the message they tried to convey. But, Nehemiah sets the stage for the entire rest of the story, "Then I answered them, and said unto them, the God of heaven, he will prosper us; therefore, we his servants will arise and build; but you have no portion, nor right, nor memorial, in Jerusalem." (Nehemiah 2:20) He establishes who is in charge, "the God of heaven." He establishes who is responsible for their success, "he will prosper us." He establishes they are putting action to their faith, "we his servants will arise and build." He establishes the covenant they have with God and that covenant is with His people, "You have no portion, nor right." Finally, he establishes their inheritance with God, "You have no memorial", meaning there is no remembrance of you but as the children of Israel He remembers us as the child of promise to our Father Abraham and this city belongs to us.

Sanbalat continues his attack against Nehemiah when he heard they were building the wall because it made him mad, so he mocked the Jews. Tobiah joins him by making fun of their building efforts saying a fox could knock the wall over. Nehemiah takes it to God, Chapter 4:4, "Hear, O our God; for we are despised: and turn their reproach upon their own head…" Do not cover their iniquity, don't blot out their sin because they have tried to demoralize the builders and provoke you. The reaction of Nehemiah and the people is found in 4:6, "so we built the wall."

Remember, this chapter is titled, "Weapons of Warfare and Take Captive Thoughts", we find what the Israelite's thoughts were in the second half of this verse, "for the people had a mind (what was deep in their heart, who they really were) to work." They used the weapon of prayer that called on God to act contrary to the enemy's effort multiple times in this fourth chapter. They applied faith by doing something about it, they continued to work, they persisted in doing what God had set them at task to do. They relied on the weapon of covenant that was established by God. They remembered their inheritance and reminded God they belonged to Him. They did not dwell upon the worthless efforts of the enemy. They kept renewing their minds with these weapons. The more you think in covenant and inheritance, acting in faith, the more secure you become in the knowledge of the Covenant God.

Let's realize that this wall was a mess, rubble if you will. For the people to maneuver over the terrain and torn down walls was a major effort. They had to clear things out of the way even before they started laying the blocks. This is extremely hard work, taxing, even for the most fit person. It is one thing when life is going well, you feel good and strong. Everything is going your way. Handling a small problem is nothing, right? Well what about that day where work isn't going well, family problems at home, maybe someone is really sick, or you have a Mother-in-law issue, or one of your relatives has passed away? Add to it financial difficulties that have persisted for months and you seem to have to cram twenty-two hours of life into ten hours. In other words, you are tired and maybe even weary. At this point, fear and doubt stand up and take center stage in your thoughts. You become concerned about how your life is going, or even perhaps your well-being. What about those you love, how is it going to affect them?

This is absolutely the situation facing Nehemiah and the Jews as they were building the wall. Working from sunup to sundown, being threatened while they were at work. Concerned for their well-being and for those around them that they loved. Each time the enemy mounted a threat, they turned to God, and in their weariness they did what was written in Chapter 4:14, "And I (Nehemiah) looked, and rose up, and said unto the nobles, and to the rulers, and to the rest of the people, be not ye afraid of them: remember the Lord, which is great and terrible, and fight for your brethren, your sons, and your daughters, your wives and your houses." They captured those thoughts of fear and intimidation brought by the enemy pushing those thoughts out of their hearts and minds. They remembered their Covenant God who is great and terrible, that he is the Most High and there is no other god. Then they turned from a defensive stance to an offensive position, they fought for their families, their sons and daughters, their wives, and homes. Don't dwell on what you don't have, don't look at what the enemy says to bring fear, get your mind right – put your thoughts on God, who he is, and what he is able to do. But rise up and do every day. Give God something to work with, act in faith. [24]

---

[24] If Nehemiah had done nothing while in the Palace at Shushan, no prayer, no fasting, no repenting, no trusting in the God of Covenant, this wall would have not been built. The Jews at Jerusalem would have remained a reproach. But he did spend time seeking God with his whole heart and mind. Nehemiah looked around and saw a people who were tired, burdened and he rose up, encouraging the people to move forward away from fear and focusing on the important things like your family, Nehemiah 4:14.

Remember Elijah how he took thought on the fear and intimidation used by Jezebel, how God prevailed in the end, as he always will, but it cost Elijah the opportunity of not finishing the task. Sanballat, Tobiah and Gesham resorted to using tactics that would cause the people to fear because fear can be crippling and cause us to not be fruitful. When Nehemiah in chapter 6:10 went to the house of Shemaiah, this man offered him what sounded like a reasonable solution for the safety of his life. Go to the temple and shut yourself in for your safety because they will come to kill you tonight. Nehemiah explains that it is not his life that he is concerned with and refused the offer. Nehemiah perceived or recognized and understood that this man was not sent by God because he had encapsulated his offer of safety with fear for his life (Nehemiah 6:10-13). Shemaiah was hired by the enemy to get Nehemiah to act in fear and by acting in fear he would sin against God. Actions taken out of fear are not of faith and fear does not come from God, but the enemy is always thrusting fear at us, love is the force that overcomes fear and God is love and he has no fear, period.

Adam's actions caused fear to come and fear is the direct attack of Satan to disrupt us from a Spirit filled life. Fear is the best effort our flesh can conjure up as a means to protect ourselves. Why are you afraid of the dark? Because you are concerned about your safety and your flesh does not comprehend what it does not see or know. It is impossible to please God without faith (Hebrews 6:11). When we act in fear or take thoughts of fear we most certainly are not living in faith and this is what causes us to sin against God (Romans 14:23). As stated earlier Nehemiah was not concerned for his "self" so he was able to recognize that fear for life is a lie from the devil.

Nehemiah and the Jews built the entire wall around the entire city, clearing rubble, being prepared for war, taking care of each other and they did it in a mere 52 days. No bulldozers, no big cranes like we have today, just people with a mind to work. Unity is a mighty tool, a mighty weapon to be used against the enemy that comes against God. Unity

---

Accomplishing the task God has set before you will bring protection for your family. A walled city in those days was a prosperous city.

with each other, unity in the spirit (Ephesians 4:3) changes societies, when a nation turns to God and follows his love, he will fight for you.

Quickly look at Nehemiah 4:6 and 6:2 to determine the thought process of both sides here. The people of Israel had a "mind to work." Sanbalat and his cohorts, "thought to do mischief." Look where their thoughts were, one side was positive, moving forward, accomplishing a task. The other side was scheming, being divisive, thinking about ways to undermine, thwart, defeat, acting completely in the negative with their thoughts and conversation.

When you rise up and work, getting to the task God set before you then you will find yourself not being concerned about weariness, but you will find a supernatural strength that drives you to accomplish the task.[25] When you do this, when you turn to God and pray, when you get it so deep into your heart that it comes out in a passion, when you remember the Covenant God you will find the enemies counsel will be brought to naught by God himself. The result of this is found in Nehemiah 6:16, "…when *all* our enemies heard and saw these things, they were much cast down in their own eyes: for they perceived that this work was wrought of our God."

Trust in God. Know that He has both the outcome and the enemy in hand. When you stand and do not take the thought of fear, the enemy will lose his confidence. Push fear out, take the word of God, give God yourself without concern for your "self." When you have accomplished the task set before you it will change the outlook of your enemies.

---

[25] Do not ask the question, "Well, what is my task, what is the will of God for my life?" Instead pray, "that I may know you, that I may know your heart Father." The task before you is simple – think right thoughts about everything, love God, do good, forgive each other, build relationships that blossom with the love of Christ. Read the word of God and do those things that the word says is pleasing to him, the things that are beautiful, lovely and humbling. The more you know Him the more you know what to do, the less you become concerned with trying to accomplish a thing that, in reality, is self-promoting. When it springs up from deep inside you, as it did in Nehemiah, it will drive you to God, and you'll know it is from him. Maybe it is for your wife or your children or the job you have or possibly a nation. Do it in humility, do it for Him, do it with Him. God will prosper His word.

Jeremiah

Let's take a look at our third example and check out a man, that from his youth, spoke exactly what the God of heaven commanded him to speak. Notwithstanding, he spoke it during a time when the world was changing around him. History was setting in motion what would impact the path the entire world would follow from then to present day. An empire would be born, and this man would proclaim its sovereignty over and the resulting consequence to his nation through their disobedience to the God of Covenant. Israel was the nation, Babylon was the Empire and Jeremiah was the man who courageously spoke for God during a time of world change while enduring godly disobedience, anger, self-serving leaders, hatred, prison and attempts on his life. Israel as a nation, the leaders of the church, the King and his advisers absolutely rejected everything that Jeremiah spoke concerning the welfare of the people of Israel.

Time and again, Jeremiah conveys the message that Israel, as a nation and people, return to the Lord their God because he is their God and they are his children (Jeremiah 4:1). God subsequently points out they have a heart problem; they have a heart that is covered over by the flesh. Read these verses: Jeremiah 3:10 "… Judah has not turned unto me with her whole heart;" 4:4 "Circumcise yourselves to the Lord, and take away the foreskins of you heart…;" 9:26 "… and all the house of Israel are uncircumcised in the heart;" 11:8 "Yet they obeyed not, nor inclined their ear, but walked everyone in the imagination of their evil heart…;" 14:14 "… they prophesy unto you a false vision and divination, and a thing of naught and the deceit of their heart;" 17:9 " The heart is deceitful above all things, and desperately wicked…;" 18:12 "And they said, there is no hope: but we will walk after our own devices, and we will everyone do the imagination of his evil heart."

You see, when we reject and rebel against our God by following our own ways deceived by our flesh, our sin nature, then all that is left is an evil heart. It is who we really are inside, and it comes out in what we do and what we say. But Jeremiah always gave the people a way out because God said, "If you will turn." This is known as repentance, asking God to forgive us. But you have to make a conscious decision to take captive those thoughts that want to drive you to rejection. You have to want to cut away the flesh that fills your heart and ask God to fill it with truth and love.

Jeremiah used weapons of warfare that were most certainly tested in the most extreme conditions and hottest of fiery trials. Using the Word of God to control his thoughts. Being confident that the extreme pressure being placed upon him would not cost him his life because God said so. God would be his deliverer (Jeremiah 1:19). Fear, for Jeremiah, was eliminated, you cannot be strong and confident, speaking boldly and passionately if you are concerned about your "self." Fear will attack your flesh, self-sin nature, and cause you to weaken or lose all resolve during these trials.

Jeremiah was tasked with a passion that few in the course of history had to endure. Those that have are often written about in our history books. He was instructed early on by God himself that he would speak to the, "... nations and over the kingdoms..." (1:10), to the, "...kings of Judah, against the princes, against the priests and against the people of the land." (1:18). He was told that, "they shall fight against you..." (1:19), and fight they did. In Jeremiah 26:7-11 he stands in the court of the Lord's house and speaks exactly what God had told him to speak. He said, "You need to listen to God and if you don't you will see defeat like you did at Shiloh and you will be a curse to all nations." (paraphrased). Not a flowery, feel good speech is it? How did the priests and the people respond? Look at verse 8, "... the priests and the prophets and all the people took him, saying, thou shalt surely die." The leaders of the church, the prophets, the men who were the ones to deliver the word of the Lord to the people and even all the people standing there that day were against him, but as God had promised Jeremiah, God delivered him from the death they had thought to do to him.

Look at chapter 36 were Jeremiah hears from God again and is told to write everything down that God has spoken to him from the first day God called him until the present time. This covers quite the span of years. So, he writes it all down with this fellow named Baruch. Since Jeremiah was restricted from gong to the house of the Lord due to previous encounters at church, he has Baruch read it to the people. Well this caused quite a stir and the leaders in attendance took this word up the chain of command with it finally ending up being read to the King. What did the King do with this history of, "thus saith the Lord"? Well, he cut it up and threw it into the fire. The King wanted nothing to do with what Jeremiah had to say. [26]

So what does Jeremiah have to say about this life God has laid before him? Chapter 20:7 says, "O Lord, thou hast deceived me, and I was deceived: thou art stronger than I, and thou hast prevailed: I am in derision daily, everyone mocks me." Jeremiah writes about what his life is like, the shame, the whisperings about him, the people who want to denounce him, waiting for him to be deceived, even those who he thought of as friends were against him. This does not sound like a life any of us would be jumping at for a chance to live.

But what was in his heart? It was the Word of God! Hebrews 4:12 says, "For the word of God is quick, and powerful, and sharper than any two edged-sword, piercing even to the dividing asunder of soul and spirit, and even of the joints and marrow, and is a discerner of the thoughts and intents of the heart." Jeremiah speaks the truth of this in chapter 20:9, "Then I said, I will not make mention of him, nor speak any more in his name. *But his word was in my heart* as a burning fire shut up in my bones, and I was weary with forebearing, and I could not stay." (italics added). You cannot quench the powerful life force of the word of the living God. You cannot shut it up, you cannot hide it, you

---

[26] Many times in the Bible, the people God called to do His word, were faced with enemies. Read Psalm 38:19-20 where David speaks of the strength of his enemies and those who render evil for good. But David says, "I follow what is good." To stand in the face of adversity and continue to do good – what God commands – takes a heart and mind that continually seeks God.

cannot prevent it from performing what it was set forth to accomplish. You were created by it. Do you understand the power and weight of authority a soul who does not live for self has, that is given to them without reservation, but knows that God performs what He speaks?

Oh, you must read Lamentations chapter 3 and read it with Jeremiah's heart. He has been crushed, betrayed, hurt, bruised by God, by his fellow prophets, his leaders, and his people. *But* he remains faithful to the Word of God given to him, always faithful. He writes of the darkness he has been brought into. He writes of the travail. He writes of being hedged in and there is no way out. His paths are crooked, his prayers are shut out, he is pulled in pieces and made desolate, even his people consider him to be a laughingstock. Once again though, what is in his heart? In verse 19, he recalls, "Remembering my affliction and my misery, the wormwood and the gall. My soul has them still in remembrance, and is humbled in me." (Lamentations 3:19,20). He understands his position as a created being and in verse 21 says, "This I recall to my mind, therefore I have hope. It is of the Lord's mercies that we are not consumed, because his compassions fail not. They are new every morning: great is thy faithfulness." (Lamentations 3:22,23). The Lord is Jeremiah's portion, giving him hope. The Lord is good to those who wait and seek Him. He does not afflict willingly. Who are we to complain in light of our sins and His perfect brightness? Verse 40 reads, "Let us examine and try our ways, and turn again to the Lord. Let us lift up our heart with our hands unto God in the heavens." (Lamentations 3:40,41). Jeremiah is putting into practice the very message he is preaching to the Israelites.

We remember our heartaches, our hard times and our battles, but it should not lead us to thoughts that generate bitterness in our soul. Instead, our thoughts should be on him to give us hope, to humble us and know he is forever faithful. He is our portion, our inheritance. He is forever compassionate, full of tender loving kindnesses. In verse 55 Jeremiah tells us he, "called upon the Lord out of the low dungeon." (Lamentations 3:55). Has not everyone encountered a low point in their life? Have we not all experienced a heartache, an oppression, a depression, emotional hurts that have left us scarred? Jeremiah certainly dealt with all the above but look at what sustains him as read in verses 57 and 58. God drew near in the day Jeremiah called upon him. God told him, "Fear not." It was God who pleaded the causes of his soul. It was God who redeemed his life. He is infinite in his purpose. He is the same yesterday, today and always, yet he is unique to each of us in our very own circumstances. There is no limit to his love for us or how it may be expressed.

Jeremiah, while living through this affliction, kept his thoughts on what God said. He would think about all that was against him but would take captive those thoughts by remembering the faithfulness of God and how He loves us. In turn, knowing God said, "Fear not", he turned those accusers over into God's hands in verse 64, "Render unto them a recompence, O Lord, according to the work of their hands." (Lamentations 3:64). Stop reacting to those who bring strife into your life. Stop fighting them with the same tactics they use against you. Use the weapons of our warfare, taking captive thoughts to the obedience of Christ, speaking right and truth, thinking on good and not on our own self-justification. Fear not. Ask God to strengthen you, guide you, to give you grace, wisdom and understanding.

You say, "I have been trying to do this, but it isn't working." Remember what was going on around Jeremiah kept going on until the Israelites were taken away into captivity by the Babylonian Empire. It is not our circumstances that are to dictate who we are it is our willingness to abandon ourselves to him and him alone. It is not flesh and blood we wrestle against (Ephesians 6:12). These people were created in the image of God just as we are. Our warfare is not against each other, it is against the spiritual forces, the principalities, against powers, against the rulers of the darkness of this world, against spiritual wickedness in heavenly places. Do you want to see change from evil, self-seeking, condemning spirits? Then you must use the weapons of our warfare that

100

are not carnal but divine and mighty through God to the pulling down of strongholds (2 Corinthians 10:4,5).

God turns our hearts we don't change someone else's heart. If, however, you decide to harden your heart and remain in rebellion to our Creator, then you will most certainly find yourself fighting against God, and he will recompense to you according to the work of your hands.[27] *Do Not Fear.* Trust him to deliver you. Do not be presumptuous toward God by expecting Him to deliver you the way you want because it is not about us. It is about him.

Warfare is always a two-way street in which we obviously are engaged with the enemy but at the same time we must be constant in examining ourselves. We do so by staying in faith while exercising ourselves through application as we are taking captive our thoughts and speaking the word of God to stay in top condition spiritually (1 Timothy 4:7-10; Hebrews 5:14). If you examine yourselves with pride, you are setting yourself up for a fall (James 4:6; Proverbs 13:10 and 16:18). If, however, you examine yourself with perspective that is aligned with his word you will gain understanding.

Psalm 119:161 says, "Princes have persecuted me without a cause: but my *heart* stands in awe of your word." (italics added). Psalm 119:71 says, "It is good for me that I have been afflicted; that I might learn thy statutes." The more my thoughts fill my heart with his Word, the less pride I have, and the more understanding I gain concerning the persecutions and afflictions in my life. The less I see them as dictating my heart, the more I will know and trust a faithful loving God. If you are struggling with troubles, take time to read Psalm 119 over and over and rest (cease from labor; 2 Thessalonians 1:7). See how the Psalmist looks to the word of God for strength, comfort, perspective on God, on who his enemies are, and on what God shall do to his enemies.

---

[27] The works of our hands are the direct result (action taken) of what we express out of our hearts and minds. You do not do an evil act without it not first coming from what is in your heart. Hardened hearts are a series of thoughts that doubt, reject and disobey the commands of the Most High God by continually thinking and dwelling on those thought

You must come to a point where you say, "I believe, no matter what, I believe I am in his hands." If you are one of those who have been wearied by life, what people say about you, how you are treated, and even have thoughts of committing suicide, *Stop It*. Take captive, actively take those thoughts captive. Get up and know that no one on this earth weather, mother, father, sister, brother, friend, or someone who just wants to put you down is capable of destroying the love God has for us, life is never encapsulated in the simple moment that you are caught up in, life is ever expanding and cutting it short is a lie from the devil to prevent you from bearing fruit.

Look again at 2 Corinthians 10:5, "Casting down imaginations, and every high thing that exalts itself against the knowledge of God, and bringing into captivity every thought to the obedience of Christ." What isn't of God, what isn't of faith, what isn't of love, whatever thought we have that promotes ourselves, that brings anger, that offends knowingly, comes from our reasoning, our imagination and exalts itself above the knowledge of God. These are the things we must bring into captivity to the obedience of Christ.

What is the obedience of Christ? Jesus is the Anointed One, the Messiah, the author and finisher of our faith, the High and Lofty One, the Word. He is our High Priest able to identify with our infirmities. He is our Healer, the Great Physician. He is our intercessor, praying for us continually. He is the Son of the Living God given for us to redeem us from our falling short of the glory of God. He is our sacrifice. He is the Chief Corner Stone. He established a new covenant with us, and he will put his laws into our hearts and write them in our minds. He is grace unto us. He is this and so much more and we need to find out for ourselves all that he is till we all come to the measure of the stature of the fullness of Christ (Ephesians 4:13). Jesus did not give thought to the desires of the flesh. Obedience is the mind and the stature and the authority and the grace and peace of one who comes to do the will of him who sent me (John 6:38).

We need to know the mind of Christ to understand His obedience. Psalm 119:73-80, we are told that he hoped in the word God spoke. He knew God's judgements are right. He knew that his affliction was by his faithfulness. He knew God's merciful kindness was for his comfort. He knew that by his tender mercies he would live. He let his thoughts meditate in God's precepts. He asked that his heart be sound in God's statutes so he would not be ashamed. Obedience is a knowledge of, an understanding of, a trust in, a reliance on and a desire to commit yourself to something, or someone that comes with authority over and ownership of all that pertains to what you have been instructed to perform. You do not seek your own. You do not interfere by introducing your own thoughts or your complaints. You do what you are instructed to do.

Hebrews 5:8-9, speaks of, even though he was the Son of God he learned obedience by the things he suffered. He became the author of eternal salvation to all of us who obey.

Hebrews 2:9-10 speaks of, but we see Jesus who gave up position for us to suffer death for us.

Hebrews 10:7 speaks of, he did not seek his own way but came to do the will of God as it is written in the book about him.

Philippians 2:5-8 speaks of, he didn't think it to be robbery to be equal to God, but being equal, he made himself of no reputation, a servant in the likeness of the man he created. He humbled himself to the point of death on the cross.

Hebrews 12:2 speaks of, he endured the cross and ignored the shame.

1 Peter 2:21-22 speaks of, Christ left us an example to follow concerning how we are to act and speak.

1 Peter 4:1 speaks of, we are to arm ourselves with the same mind Christ has so our thoughts do not become corrupted with self-justification.

Romans 15:3 speaks of, for even Christ pleased not himself.

Hebrews 5:5 speaks of, so also Christ glorified not himself.

1 Corinthians 1:24 speaks of, Christ the power of God and the wisdom of God.

The obedience of Christ is the power of God, the wisdom of God. It is not self-seeking. It is not pride in achievements. It is doing the Word of God as it is written. It is living through the affliction, the circumstances, the persecution, the harassments, the anger, the hurts, the anguish, the burdens, the sufferings and punishments by the love of Christ, the love of Jesus, the love of the Holy Spirit shed abroad in our hearts, and the very love of God. It is giving all of who you are, all of the attacks, and all injustices over to a just God knowing He shall surely recompense to all according to their works. Jeremiah did this giving his heart over to the God who had called him even before he was formed and born from his Mother's womb. [28]

Jeremiah was obedient to God though all those around him disobeyed and rejected the word God gave them. He spent his entire life preaching one message, "Turn your heart back to the Lord God of Israel. If you don't then God will bring evil upon this nation." Obedience brings deliverance because God is merciful and desires to pour out love upon us (Jeremiah 18:8; 23:22; 29:10,11). Obedience

---

[28] Do not take it upon yourself to determine what a child shall become whether they be yet born or already free of the womb. Let God be God. Let us be yielded to the one who knows the end from the beginning. The one who turns our hearts. The one who sanctifies us. The one who gives life. It is our responsibility to train up or dedicate a child to the one who formed it. By teaching good. By teaching true respect. By learning not to take offense because we know we are made in his image and not the image someone may be making us out to be. Look at the confusion so many live their lives in because they do not know how to call upon the living God. Know this that nothing dead gives life. Life begets life.

results in righteousness bringing us an abundance of grace (Romans 5:19-21). Obedience to the truth purifies your souls, which leads us to being able to love one another from a pure heart (1 Peter 1:22). Obedience allows us to not conform to our old sinful self (1 Peter 1:14). Obedience gives us the ability to listen to faith, to hear it, to know (Acts 6:7; and Romans 10:17).

Jeremiah gave all of Israel for many years the choice to turn back to God and to stop the evil they were living in. Israel did not take the Word of God given to them by Jeremiah which resulted in captivity. Look at your life are you in captivity to burdens, to fear and to the worry of your circumstances? Does the bondage of a lifetime to the fear of death rob you of joy and opportunity? Does it steal your peace and contentment? Has it killed your relationships with your husband or wife, your children, or your parents and even your friends? Have the things you have strived for been destroyed (Hebrews 2:15; John 10:10)?

By turning your heart back to the Lord; by taking captive thoughts that steer your heart away from good, right, peace, hope, faith, and love; and by becoming obedient to the truth, which is being obedient to the Christ, you step into a resurrected life. You step into a deliverance. You step into mercy.

We are not all called to stand in such a face of adversity as Jeremiah was, but we are all called to take captive every thought to the obedience of Christ. For many of us that is adversity enough. Jeremiah stood amongst the onslaught of discouragement, anger, hatred, lies, physical pain and mental anguish yet did battle with the weapons of warfare by taking captive his thoughts to the obedience of Christ. By trusting God to deliver him and not depending on his "self," willing to despise the shame people placed upon him because he knew the truth (Hebrews 12:2).

In John chapter 11 we have the story of Lazarus, the brother of Mary and Martha, becoming ill. This news was brought to Jesus, but instead of dropping everything and running to the aid of Lazarus, he stayed two more days where he was at. Now everyone from Jesus' disciples to Mary and Martha and to the Jews, which were at Martha's house, were all concerned for the welfare of Lazarus. Lazarus died before Jesus even started on the journey to see his sick friend. To make a long story short, Jesus had arrived at the grave and commanded the stone to be rolled away from the grave opening. Let's get to the point here in verse 41. Jesus says, "Father, I thank you that you have heard me." He continues in verse 42, "And I *knew* that you hear me always." Have you ever spoken with someone who thinks they know what they are talking about and really don't, yet you do know? Jesus knew something the rest of the people there didn't know. They thought they knew Lazarus was dead, buried, and stinking by the time Jesus showed up. But Lazarus wasn't any of those things in the eyes of the one who knew. As Jeremiah knew the truth as we stated previously, so, too, Jesus knew the truth and more importantly he knew his Father always hears him. We've got to know He hears us, else, what good would it be for us to take captive our thoughts to the obedience of Christ. When we take captive our thoughts to the obedience of Christ, we are placing these thoughts under the blood Jesus gave for the redemption of our sins. His crucifixion and shedding of the life force, his blood, is what washes our thoughts clean (Leviticus 17:11). If the thought comes out clean, then it is from God. If it does not come out clean, good, and pure then we bind that thought up and call it to fall to the ground void (1 Samuel 3:19). This is warfare. If this is what we are doing, then we may certainly know that our Father in Heaven hears us. Anytime you are involving the shed blood of his only begotten Son that he gave to pay the sacrifice for us, you can surely bet he wants to listen to what we are saying. He hears us!

Let us bring this into our personal daily lives to see how taking captive thoughts to the obedience of Christ impacts us today. First, the warfare we are waging occurs between us and Satan's demonic forces. Second, it is the thoughts between us and our God that dictate the outcome of many of our situations. Satan has demonic forces that follow people around and gather information sometimes going back generations. We find ourselves battling against God when we serve the things of this world satisfying ourselves. When we begin to take a thought, let's say about taking a drug, and the first time that thought occurs, we may dismiss it until it comes back again. This time, we might add a little reasoning to it, maybe even softening it a little. Then an opportunity seems to pop up out of nowhere, and we might add to that thought a little justification. This process continues until that thought enters your heart and in what you have determined as an innocent "let's just try this for the fun of it, nothing will happen just doing it once" soon becomes a regular reoccurring I'm-taking-control-of-you part of your life. Satan and his demonic forces expose us to those thoughts, which are soon followed by a lie, and once the thought is in your heart, it now becomes your thought justifying and serving yourself, and now we find ourselves battling against God because these are not the thoughts he told us to think on. No matter if it is drugs, or pornography, or alcohol, or food, or sports, or gambling, or education, or our job, or our business, or desiring someone else, or arguments in our marriage, or thinking about an abortion, or losing our temper because we are frustrated, it all follows taking that first thought. No one ever became an addict by not trying something for the first time, and we all know the first thoughts we had before we did something for the first time and how we justified the following actions. None of us ever came out of it by not admitting it was devouring our lives. When the original action becomes a habit or addiction then we have succumbed to the lies and deceits of Satan and his demonic forces. He is always seeking someone whose thoughts were not taken captive and looks to devour you to kill your life.[29]

---

[29] As you begin to dwell on a thought, rehearsing it if you will, you begin to reason, in other words, you are trying to gain a mental perception, trying to see how this thought fits or plays out in realities. When you begin rehearsing these thoughts in conversation with someone else, it turns into complaining, and when you rehearse it over and over in your mind, it turns into murmuring. In Luke 5, we have the story where Jesus is in a house healing people, and a group of men open a hole in the roof to let down a friend who is on a stretcher. Jesus sees their faith and tells the man his sins are forgiven him, which doesn't settle well with the Pharisees. They begin to reason (think) about

The more Satan injects thoughts, or promotes occurrences in your life that get you to take more thoughts and spend more time looking at that thought, the more this becomes a stronghold in your life. Satan is always going to expose you to things that affect your flesh. Things that make you feel comfortable, prideful, satisfying. He wants you to feel good about lying to yourself and to others. About patting yourself on the back for accomplishments. About preconceived ideas about family, classmates, co-workers and friends or people of different color or nationalities.

Take the time right now to reread 2 Corinthians 10:4. For the weapons of our warfare are not of our flesh, our carnal sinful nature, but they are mighty through God to the pulling down of strongholds. Essentially when we make a conscious decision to give us, our selves, over to God, than through God, we are able to begin to take captive every thought to the obedience of Christ. Now you are placing these thoughts under God's authority, and this brings deliverance. Satan is walking about as a roaring lion seeking whom he may devour (1 Peter 5:8). When you give a thought an opportunity to continue, Satan will seize upon that moment to steer you closer to those things that will destroy you. You will find yourself inexplicably being drawn to that drink, that pornography, that gambling bet that will lead to debt. You will find it easier to complain about your job, or your husband, or wife, or your family, or the government, or how you look physically, or what someone said about you. When this occurs, you may know beyond a shadow of a doubt you are being devoured by Satan. Once again, though, Satan is not greater than God, he has already been judged and his end is already written. Jesus paraded this guy around as a defeated being, and he took the keys of death and hell away from him. Our weapons are mighty because they have already worked on Satan. Jesus

---

what Jesus just said and how it fits with their religious laws. Jesus, being aware of their reasoning, asks a piercing question in Luke 5:22 "Why are you reasoning in your hearts?" If you plan on reasoning God or trust or faith or love, you will certainly fall short. Because God is our trust, he is our faith and God is love, and you cannot out reason the Living God, the Ancient of Days.

proved those weapons. They work. Take your thoughts captive to the obedience of Christ and start getting back to life as God purposed it.

Common Threads

Now let's wrap this chapter up by looking at the common threads that exist in the examples of Elijah, Nehemiah, and Jeremiah. All three men knew the word God had spoken. All three men were tasked by God to accomplish his word. All three men were confronted with fear.

Knowing the Word of God is tantamount to knowing God. The Word of God was given to these men and became scripture that we might experience the power of God's Word lived through the lives of these men.

Being tasked by God to accomplish his Word is not held to the Old Testament alone. It is vital to this planet today. Don't get caught up in thinking you have to call down fire from heaven to show people God. Look at the task we are given today. We are to love one another. We are to love our brother. We are to have unity of the Spirit. We are to love our neighbor as our self. We are to love God with all our heart, with all our soul and with all our mind (Matthew 22:37-40). What would our lives be like, what would our society be like, and what would our world be like, if we would perform this task set before us? When you do this, when you put your heart, your soul, and your mind to perform the task of accomplishing his Word by the giving of yourself and by doing good and right, by taking captive your thoughts and resisting the devil, there is no limit to the fulness of God you will experience.

Each of these men confronted fear, and we are able to see the results of how each man handled it. When we look at ourselves becoming concerned for what is going to happen to us, we lose all power over fear. When our thoughts feed our heart with the Word of God, the love of God, the grace of God, the mercy of God, the promises of God and the peace of God, than through covenant this is what is going to come out of our heart. Perfect mature love casts out fear (1 John 4:18).

By taking captive every thought to the obedience of Christ and by using the weapons of our warfare that are mighty through God, we give honor to God. We give to all around us the presence of God, which is giving God glory because it demonstrates it is of his hand not ours. We have become dependent upon the sovereign God (1 Timothy 1:17).

CHAPTER 6

TAKE PEACE AND GIVE PEACE

"Peace I leave with you, my peace I give unto you: not as the world gives, give I unto you. Let not your heart be troubled, neither let it be afraid."

-John 14:27

Nearly all of us walking on this earth often, and at various times in our life, find peace a very elusive thing. We become mired in the conflicts of life while being stuck in our worries and cares of things that too often seem out of our control. "She said this about me," or "Did you see how he is treating me," or "Look at what that politician is doing." Every aspect of our lives has opportunity, events, and people that may, or could impede the peace we have. What really is peace? How do we obtain that peace Jesus spoke of in the opening verse above? How do we lose our peace? Who is peace? What develops peace for us to live in? Let's take a look at peace in a way we may never have thought of before.

Peace is a thought, or decision, a place, a condition, an event, or circumstance where there is an absence of conflict. The Miriam Webster Dictionary describes peace as in this manner:

1. a state of tranquility or quiet.

2. freedom from disquieting, or oppressive thoughts, or emotions.

3. harmony in personal relationships; and

4. a state, or period of mutual accord between governments.

To better understand peace, we will look at conflict so we may see both sides. What is conflict? What is it that sets people at odds with each other? Conflict occurs when I as an individual, organization, people or government determine that my self-interests and ideals are to be placed over another without regard to the other sides concerns, welfare, or outcome. This has often led us to broken relationships, offenses, fights, and even wars. Conflict, when handled incorrectly, most certainly strains peace and may even end peace. History will offer up the proof that conflict can become uncontrolled removing all elements of peace until peace is fought for. Something to remember here is that no conflict lasts forever. There is always an end to it. Peace always finds its way back.

Look at how the world gives peace. It is always with conditions, compromises, and often temporary license. It is never enduring. It is always a "You do this, and I'll do that so we can prevent conflict." These may work for a while until one side determines once again their self-interests are not being met. Peace, as the world gives, is generally fake in its purpose. It may look good on the outside, but it is almost always hollow.

Satan is the master of conflict and in this book of *Give and Take* we see how he uses it to his advantage. Satan gives us lies to deceive us when once we take the thoughts he interjects and get them down into our hearts. We begin to act out the lies stored up in our heart, and we become divisive. Once we become divisive, Satan is free to steal our peace (John 10:10). He is a thief. A thief takes what is not rightfully his. A thief rarely knows the true value of what he is taking. A thief takes without regard of the owner's sense of worth or wellbeing. A thief cares for nothing of the personal result, or outcome to the owner. A thief isn't willing to work for gain. He is lazy wanting only to gain from other's efforts. Oftentimes, a thief is driven by fear of desperation, or by his wants and desires.

Bear in mind Satan is not dividing his own house, but he is dividing ours. He wants us to be in conflict within ourselves, with our family, our community and even our people (Matthew 12:22-29; Luke 11:14-22). Division is such a sad tool Satan uses. It brings with it offense, anger, unhappiness, sorrow, bitterness, and the like which kills relationships and destroys community amongst us. It will evolve into hatred which is simply uncontrolled and unchecked emotion that never has a good outcome for either side of the matter. Will your anger, unhappiness, sorrow, bitterness, and hatred solve the problem, resulting in peace?

A kingdom, or house divided amongst itself has lost concern for others in its ranks. Instead, it focuses on the conflict. Often being involved in conflict, we ourselves are unsure of how we think, or perceive ourselves, let alone the other side. A distinction must be made here to understand conflict. If the conflict is internal, and it tears you between promoting yourself, or acting in a humble manner, than you must take those thoughts captive to the obedience of Christ and wash them under the blood of Jesus. You will know the right and the good, giving God the glory and honor when you humble yourself under the mighty hand of God. If the conflict is external involving peoples, organizations, and nations while it contains oppression removing freedom (even in small seemingly insignificant ways at first), false accusations, slanders, boasting, and intimidation while calling that which is evil as good, and conversely calling that which is good as evil, than this, most certainly is a time for us to do warfare (Isaiah 5:20). Not fighting against each other, which only empowers division but do warfare against the principalities, the powers, the rulers of the darkness of this world and spiritual wickedness in heavenly places (Ephesians 6:12). In truth, it is time to fight for peace through the word of God, by trust in God, by the grace of God, and the love of God utilizing the gifts of the Holy Spirit and the weapons of our warfare, which are supernatural (God inspired) and taking captive our thoughts to the obedience of Christ. Resisting the devil in our thoughts and actions causing him to flee. The more people resist the devil, the easier it is for peace to come in (James 4:7; 1 Peter 5:9). By not seeking our own satisfaction for selfish desires and by giving God our desires, we will take control of our thoughts, which doesn't give the devil an opportunity. This resistance to the devil will spread to others when they begin to realize they are covered by God's grace and mercy. A soft answer, gentle in its nature, turns away anger, or wrath, or rage (Proverbs 15:1). This kind of attitude builds spreading from person to person, from community to community, because Satan is being resisted by our spirit, which is moving with the Spirit of God, and this brings unity. Unity is the driving force behind every victory. When your spirit is yielded to the Holy Spirit, unity is achieved, thereby spreading the fruit of the Holy Spirit.

You may be thinking *I have to do something to defeat this conflict*. If you move in your own strength, your own initiative, your own emotions then you are simply adding to the conflict. You move when God tells you to move. When it aligns with the word of God and when you have peace about what you are about to do - not being conflicted in your thoughts (I Peter 3:10-12). Do not deceive yourself and structure the scriptures to accomplish the outcome you desire. Know this, God is not overwhelmed by you, or the other side of the conflict. He is able to deliver.

Conflict is an opportunity for all involved. It should *not* be an opportunity for us to choose bitterness, frustration, hatred, and anger. It should be used as an opportunity for us to turn to the Living God in trust and faith, in hope and love, in peace and grace, knowing we are in his hands. Remember when you were first in love with someone, there was no conflict. You were both just taken away by each other being lost in love. Does this mean when a conflict arises in your relationship that you are no longer in love? Not if you handle the conflict in love, not selfishly, or pridefully. Bearing all things. Believing in each other. Hoping in each other. Enduring each other. Living in a relationship this way will result in peace. Conflict should not be the end of a thing but a stepping-stone in the process of growth. Learn from it, develop better foundations from it, and continue in life from it. But do it with Christ, with the Holy Spirit, and with God the Father. [30]

If conflict is to be resolved not temporarily but in an everlasting way, we need to have the eyes of our understanding opened (Ephesians 1:17-18). We need to see, or perceive, draw a mental perception, of how conflict steals our peace. Take a look at Matthew 13 and the "Parable of the Sower". A story is given to us by Jesus that has great depth to it yet is given in a manner that allows people to relate to it. A sower goes forth to sow. When you want to plant seed, you must sow your seed to the soil. Seeds don't grow when left in the package. As the sower is broadcasting the seeds, they fall to the ground with some falling beside the roadway, some falling upon the rocky stony ground, some falling amongst the thorns, and some falling on the good ground.

This is known as a parable. Jesus spoke in this manner because in order to grasp the true meaning of a story like this you need to gain an understanding. The disciples ask Jesus why he speaks to the people in parables. He answers them by telling them "Because it is given to you to know [*understand*] the mysteries of the kingdom of heaven." (Matthew

---

[30] A.B. Simpson, Days of Heaven on Earth; May 3

My peace I give unto you - John 14:27

Here lies the secret of abiding peace – God's peace. We give ourselves to God and the Holy Spirit takes possession of our hearts. It is indeed "Peace, peace." But it is at this precise point that the devil begins to interfere, and he does it through our thoughts, diverting or distracting them as the occasion requires.

This is the time to prove the sincerity of our consecration and singleness of our hearts. If we truly desire His presence more than anything, we will turn away from every conflicting thought and look steadily up to Jesus. But if we desire the gratification of our impulses more than his presence, we will yield to the passionate word, or the frivolous thought, or the sinful diversion. Then when we come back, our Shepherd has gone, and we wonder why our peace has departed.

Failure occurs often in some insignificant thing – usually a thought or word. The soul that would not fear to climb a mountain may actually stumble over a straw.

The real secret of perfect rest is to be jealously, habitually occupied with Jesus.

13:11, italics added). Then Jesus adds "but to those outside of us, it is not given." Now he goes on to explain this comment and substance of the parable.

Those who have an open heart - willing to see and hear - are given more because they perceive mentally and spiritually what God is accomplishing because they hunger and thirst after righteousness by believing (Matthew 5:6). Those who shut out the work of God get whatever they do have taken away. The prophet Isaiah spoke of this long before the time Jesus gave us this parable (Isaiah 6:9,10). Just what is he saying to us here? We hear, and we see, but we don't understand. Hearing is an active occasion for us. How many times are we involved in a conversation hearing someone speak, but we really aren't listening? There isn't a husband and wife in the world that hasn't partaken of this in some degree. Seeing: is us choosing what we are looking at mentally and physically both purposely and accidentally. Listening: is the active part.

The Hebrews, during the time of the Bible, packed a word with depth in its meaning. Today we have shallow words often taking them at face value only. The words hearing and seeing spoken here by Jesus go a bit deeper than face value. These terms give a meaning on how or what a person is taking in, how they are perceiving a thing, and what mental thoughts we have formulated. Consequently, what we are allowing into our hearts. The people Jesus is telling the parable to, as well as any who have read or heard this parable, have hearts that have become dull. They have taken into their hearts and minds the politics, the religion, the jobs, the things that satisfy their desires. The compromising, self-serving, just leave me alone, attitudes that sound good but fall short of God's commands. They actively shut their eyes to the words and miracles of Jesus by never coming to believe. They marveled at how this man spoke such sound doctrine and came to him for the miracles so they could be healed but that was mostly self-serving (Matthew 13:15 and John 6:26). Had they opened their eyes and ears to gain the proper mental thoughts, perceptions, and attitudes they would have been converted, healed, and forgiven of their sins (Matthew 13:15; Mark 4:12). Their hearts would have been open to the knowledge that Jesus was the Kingdom of God amongst them, within them (Luke 17:21; Matthew 12:28; 13:24; Galatians 1:16). God has spiritual laws created inside you to know Him.

During the time of Jesus, the Roman Empire had plenty of politics being played out, having no shortage of religions, with people making compromises and seeking to make gain for themselves. Conflict was on all sides in every arena. Rome was trying to maintain governance over a conquered people. Freedoms were being throttled. Religions were trying to remain relevant. Peace was present for those willing to compromise, but it was fragile at its best. To others, peace was elusive because of the bondages they were under. Today's times are no different. We need to stop looking at the world through eyes that are closed to the things of spiritual concern. We need to stop hearing the negative compromising attitudes and listen to the power of the truth of the gospel of Jesus the Christ.[31]

Back to the parable of the sower and the explanation Jesus gives us, which will render to us the everlasting way to resolve conflict. That will deliver peace through our understanding. You will find it is a work of the Holy Spirit. Jesus says, "Hear then the parable of the sower." He is saying if we, with an open heart and mind, gain understanding of what this means, we will be able to perceive and see how God works in and through the Word.

In Matthew 13:19, he starts out "when any one hears," This opens the whole parable to all of us. Anyone means *any-one*. This is not closed off to a specific few but is open to all. When anyone hears the word of the Kingdom and does not understand it, the wicked one comes and

---

[31] A false prophet brings his message from a deceived heart. He has deceived himself by allowing his thoughts to focus on what is comfortable to him. These thoughts promote him, satisfying him. They are willing to deceive any who are not rooted in love. They will be rejected by the Most High God because they do not speak His words but their own. They have hardened hearts that have become dull to the Truth

snatches it away out of his heart. This is seed which is sown by the roadside. When you see the berm along the road, anything that lies there is easily seen, open, and unprotected. The ground here is either compacted, or covered with asphalt. If I sow seed here, it is uncovered, open, and vulnerable, easily devoured by the birds. Our heart is the soil, if it is hard, and the seed, which is the Word of God, falls here even before it is given a chance to grow, it is snatched away. The word used here for "snatch," or catches away is aggressive in nature. It is as a thief that steals outright, openly, not in hiding, not concerned whether anyone sees, or cares about it (biblehub.com Strong's 726 *harpazo*). A hardened heart is difficult to penetrate, easy to steal what joy and peace you may have.

The seed which fell on the stony ground and quickly springs up doesn't have the soil required to take root in. Stoney ground has gaps and crevices for the seed to fall into so the birds will not be able to get to the seed to eat it immediately. Being hid from the evil one, it springs up quickly bringing joy with it, but because there is not enough sufficient soil to sustain it, when the sun beats down on it, what has grown will wither away. Soil must be moist - full of nutrients and minerals to sustain growth. Stoney places give the roots, no place to draw strength from. Our roots are our faith, and faith is of God, authored by Jesus, and moistened by the peace and love of the Holy Spirit. Take away faith, and you will most certainly wither. Hard times, persecutions, and afflictions will come to all of us, and if we don't contend with them in faith, they become very difficult to endure.

Seed sown amongst the thorns will struggle and compete for growth. Thorns and weeds grow in the corners of the field and areas not well cultivated allowing them to choke out the growth of the seed. The soil may have been prepared, but weeds grow fast in prepared soil. Ask any farmer. They will tell you the weeds always seem to grow faster than the seed sown. Anyone who may have a heart that wants to hear the word of God but doesn't really trust God, or allows things to enter their life getting caught up in what this world offers will increase the opportunity to allow themselves to be deceived. When this happens, the Word of God in your life gets choked out, and you end up not growing to maturity, thus producing little to no fruit, which is a reflection of the amount of joy and peace you may be missing out on in life.

Good soil is prepared it is ploughed and disked with plenty of water, nutrients, and fertilizers. It covers the seed and gives place for the roots to sink deep into while pulling those nutrients and moisture from it. It enjoys the warmth of the sun. Seed sown here gets cultivated to remove the weeds. When all of this comes together, the seed dies to itself and becomes what it was intended to be. It grows to maturity and produces fruit. It is no longer a seed but fully grown producing more seed to grow more of its kind.

The seed in this parable is the Word of God, and it is sown in all places whether it be along the wayside, the stony places, good soil, and even amongst the thorns. No matter if you have a hardened, dull heart, or a heart that has stony crevices, or you are caught up in the cares of this world that choke out the Word, or if you have prepared your heart, being humbled, willing to accept the sown Word; the Word is preached to all.

There are, however, some similarities amongst the places where the seed is sown. First, it all starts with hearing. Each place the seed was sown on the ground, those people heard the Word. Second, each place the seed was sown, upon hearing, received the word, it came into their thinking, their mind. The differences are the conditions and thoughts of the heart from being hard to being well prepared. Understanding, or the way we perceive what we have heard, determines the difference. If your heart is hardened by life that has been beaten upon by the wicked one, you may begin to soften by turning to forgiveness and ask the Most High God for understanding of the word. If you turn and repent, he will forgive you and heal you. By helping my dad farm land, I am able to attest to the fact that even hard ground can be broken up and planted to produce a crop. This option of turning to God for forgiveness is always available to all of us.

You will find that in all places the seed is sown, there are elements of conflict. From birds snatching away what was sown to the heat of the sun withering the growth to the thorns choking out the growth to good soil that establishes deep roots to weather the wind and storms and dry seasons. The "Parable of the Sower" leads us to what this chapter was intended for - peace. A hardened heart is not peaceful. A heart with no depth of soil may experience joy and peace at times but quickly loses it when the troubles of the day arise. A heart that doesn't trust God but worries about the cares of this world, or tries to find its happiness in riches and passion will find peace elusive and fleeting. But a heart that receives the Word and gains understanding that this Word of God is life and peace will enjoy the trust of the God of peace.

The Culmination of the Preparation

The latter heart here produces fruit in varying amounts. Fruit is the culmination of the preparation of the seed. A seed does not have to be trained on what it takes to grow and bring forth life. This is already in it. This is the work of the Holy Spirit. Galatians 5:22-23 tells us what kind of fruit we are to be producing. The fruit of love, joy, peace, patience, gentleness or kindness, goodness, faith, meekness, temperance or self-control. These are the seeds of the word of God. This is who the Holy Spirit is. When you have good soil, these are the seeds sown into it. This is the fruit that the seeds are to produce in us. Matter of fact, these are the seeds sown in all places, the roadside, the stoney places and even amongst the thorns. Look at your heart and ask yourself, "Why don't I want to grow love in my heart? Why don't I want to grow and produce peace and joy in my heart? Why don't I want to produce patience and gentleness and goodness? Why don't I want faith that others may harvest? Why wouldn't I want to produce self-control over all areas of my life being steadfast not moved by impulses and emotions?"

Jesus, the Word of God, gives us the seeds of love, the seeds of joy, the seeds of peace and patience and gentleness and goodness and faith and meekness and self-control. The Holy Spirit who gives us the fruit is all of these. He produces after His kind. Won't you be the soil He plants these seeds in? When we live in the Spirit these are the seeds given to us to produce. When we walk in the Spirit we are tending the garden, cultivating it with all carefulness allowing the seeds given to us by Jesus through the Holy Spirit to grow and prepare more fruit.[32] It is time to take the seeds of the Word of God and put them into the soil of your heart and grow.

Do not think you can shorten the arm of the Lord. This is the work of the Holy Spirit. This is his fruit. Be the one willing to struggle pushing up through the soil. Be the one who, when the rains are late, sinks your roots of faith deeper in the Holy Spirit. Be the one who stands firm when the winds and storms blow. Be the one who produces fruit some an hundred-fold, some sixty-fold, and some thirty-fold. Mature fruit produces more seed, seed for sowing (Galatians 6:7-10).

We opened this chapter with John 14:27.

"Peace I leave with you, my peace I give unto you: not as the world gives, give I unto you. Let not your heart be troubled, neither let it be afraid."

The "Parable of the Sower" is about giving. Sowing is giving. Let Jesus sow His peace, the Holy Spirit, into our hearts. Do not let the world sow its weeds in your heart. Take of the Holy Spirit and all that He jealously desires to give you. When fruit is produced, we are able

---

[32] A couple of things to think about: (1) Remember weeds come from seeds also. Be careful how you judge or what opinions you express because you may not be sowing the seeds that give life. A condescending attitude or an intentionally harsh word with the sole purpose of injury are certainly weed seeds that may grow and choke out life. Even saying those often-spoken discouraging words that affect a loved one does not promote life. (2) It is better to repent and ask for forgiveness beginning to break up the hardened ground than to reject the word of the Living God. It would be better to produce a thirty-fold harvest then none at all.

to take the fruit and use it to our benefit. Reaping is taking. Fruit is for the taking, giving us sustenance to live by and giving seed back to the sower. When we sow the seeds of peace and love, patience and goodness, the seeds of the Word of God we are then able to partake in the fruit of the Spirit. Faith is a producer of peace. Jesus is our faith. Seeds sown in faith will produce peace. When we don't have faith, we have rebellion. Rebellion is not believing God will fight for us. It is not believing he is able. This leads to conflict in our thoughts, our hearts, and our circumstances. This most certainly leads us to not having peace in our lives (Deuteronomy 1:27-30; 9:23; 10:12,17).

In John 14 we see God gave us Jesus and Jesus is in the Father and the Father is in the Son. We see Jesus' time to return to the Father has come. We see Jesus' desire is to not leave us without a Comforter, a Helper. We see Him praying to the Father for us that the Father will give us another Comforter. We see it is the Spirit of Truth. We see the Comforter is the Holy Ghost. We see Jesus, whose comfort is the Holy Spirit, gives us his peace. Which of us has not had a help, or comfort that has not brought them some element of peace? This is what Jesus had. He had peace amongst threats and oppositions. The peace he is giving us is his fruit of the Holy Spirit. Our peace is the Holy Ghost.

Faith is a seed that produces fruit. The peace Jesus left us is in the similitude of his faith. This is the work of the Holy Spirit in Jesus. Jesus had peace because his faith caused him to be at rest in the Holy Spirit.

Love is a seed given by the Holy Spirit. The love of God is shed abroad in our hearts by the Holy Spirit which is given to us from God (Romans 5:5). Are you seeing the pattern develop here? God is our Creator; everything lives and moves and has its being in Him (Acts 17:28). We have the love of God. We have Jesus, the word of God. We have the Holy Spirit who is our peace, our love, and all of them are together giving us life. We have the opportunity of being born again, not in body but in spirit, to this life through love (I Peter 1:22-23). Even a hardened heart may be reborn from the corruptible seed of hardness, anger, hatred and unforgiveness to an incorruptible seed of peace, joy in the Holy Ghost and Love.

John 7:37-39 has Jesus crying out, "If any man thirst, let him come unto me, and drink." This thirst is for more, more than who I am now. More than what I was. This thirst is for the truth, the comfort of the Holy Spirit. It comes first by glorifying Jesus in our hearts, humbling ourselves and recognizing him as our Savior. This river flowing from our heart waters and moistens the soil for seed upon receiving the Word Jesus. Don't stop at the Word, the seed sown, take the peace Jesus gave us, take the river of living water, the Holy Spirit, and grow and produce fruit. Listen, this principle of the seed and of sowing and of producing fruit and of reaping is all played out in Jesus himself (John 12:24). Remember in the Garden of Eden God planted. He created and prepared the soil. He planted and watered. Yet in our limited thinking we look at it as if he just planted the plants we see growing around us. He planted those and so much more. He planted plans, purposes and the principle of sowing and reaping for this world system, for the judgement of Satan and evil. He planted the plan for all mankind. Jesus is given to us as an example of this. Jesus is the Word, conceived by the Holy Ghost, watered again at his baptism, which is a receiving of the Holy Spirit and death by crucifixion, which led to his burial or representing being placed in the soil (Matthew 3:16; Romans 6:4). No seed lives unto itself. When planted, it must die to itself in order to grow into what it is to be. John 16:7 Jesus says, "it is important that I go away," this is talking about his death, "Then I will send the Holy Spirit to you" (paraphrased). This is the fruit bearing. We have, through His death and resurrection, the ability to take the fruit given us and enjoy peace that is a result of that fruit.

Neither Give Place to the Devil

Ephesians 4:27 tells us to not give place, or opportunity to the devil. We can find an example of this in the story of Job. When you study Job, do not look at the ordeal he endured. Iinstead, look at the structure and plan of God's Sovereignty over both the life of Job and the involvement of Satan. The story begins when Satan showed up one day in the presence of the Lord along with the sons of God, and the Lord asked him where he was coming from. Satan responded he had been walking and roaming around on the earth. In Job 1:8, the Lord asks, "Have you considered my servant Job...?" In the center column of my King James Bible it reads "Hast though set thy heart on...? In other words, God already knew what was in Satan's heart. He knew Satan had been looking at Job (Luke 16:15). Satan saw a hedge of protection the Lord had placed around Job and questioned if the prosperity Job were blessed with be removed, then how faithful would Job be? [33]

The Lord said, "Have at it." The day came when Job lost his plowing oxen, the herds of sheep, the camels, his sons, and his daughters, not to mention all the servants that were slain at each event. Job's livelihood was dissolved in a day. His family, the fruit of his loins, was taken away in a day. Satan brought conflict to Job's life. This impacted his future, the future of those families that worked for him as servants, and those who practiced business with him. This is how Satan works by bringing loss. You say, "But God allowed it." We will find out as we go deeper into this story why God gave permission to Satan to do this destructive behavior when we look closer at what was in Job's heart. Nevertheless, through all of this, the faithfulness of Job showed through. Job 1:21, "...the Lord gave and the Lord hath taken away, blessed be the name of the Lord."

A second time occurs where Satan comes before the Lord, this time questioning Job's character by asking to attack his body. Surely, if Job

---

[33] Our Father in Heaven, our Creator, already knows what is in our heats, our thoughts. He created us knowing everything about us, and he even knows Satan and what is in his heart as well because he created him as well. Do you not think that he is unable to set a hedge of protection around us? By forgiveness He has set us as righteous before him and this becomes a hedge of protection. When we give ourselves over to the doubts and thoughts of unbelief, we essentially give place to the devil or to explain it another way, we allow Satan to climb over the hedge of protection that the Lord has set about us (John 10:2, 9,16).

is wracked with pain, he will curse God. The Lord says, "Have at it again only do not take his life." Next thing you know Job is full of boils from the bottom of his feet to the top of his head. If you have ever experienced a boil, or known of someone who has, they are painful, causing discomfort, and grotesque to gaze upon. The boils on the bottom of his feet would have caused mobility to be extremely difficult. The boils on the rest of his body would have made it nearly impossible to sit, or become comfortable. The boils on his head and face would have brought a loathsome response from those who associated with him. Once again, Job's faithfulness showed up in chapter 2:10, "… shall we receive good at the hand of God, and shall we not receive evil? In all this did not Job sin with his lips." He demonstrated wisdom by not speaking against the Most High during this ordeal.

So, what is this? Why would Satan want to take on someone whom God suggests is a perfect mature man, who hates evil and fears, or reveres God (Job 2:3)? The Lord even said, "… that there is none like him in the earth…". Wow, that is quite the compliment. No one like him in the earth. This made him well known and people looked to him for wisdom, and he was considered the greatest of all the men of the East. Look how we revere those around us today most of them scarcely with a spoonful of the wisdom Job had. We look only to some simple accomplishment and make them to be greater than they are.

Well, we begin to see the answer take shape starting in chapter 3 when Job opened his mouth and began speaking from his thoughts and his heart beginning to downplay the day of his birth. We can sense a twinge of self-pity here. By the time he gets to the end of the chapter, he has really laid out the case for poor me why was I ever born. In verses 25 and 26, we start to get past the self-pity and reach the crux of the matter. "I feared a fear, and it came upon me." (Center Column). "I was not in safety, neither had I rest, neither was I quiet; yet trouble came." The fear that he gave place to lowered the hedge of protection, which in turn brings disquiet. He would not be at rest falling to concern over issues he allowed his mind to develop. We must look past what we superficially see when things occur around us. It may have sounded good to those who had come to comfort him during his plight when saying woe is me. It wasn't until he spoke the truth of the matter that the root cause came into view for us. God held Job in high esteem but knew something about Job that Job needed to face.

We are not here to judge him for his self-pity considering *every one* of us has played with self-pity at some point in our lives, many of us multiple times. We are here to look at what his thoughts had been focused on, what was in his heart. He obviously knew God and feared Him. He had the religious aspect down pat. Every time his children celebrated; Job would do a sacrifice for each child (Job 1:5). Presuming to know what was in their heart that they may have sinned and cursed God. No one knows what is in the heart of a man, save the spirit of man, which is in him (I Corinthians 2:11). If you decide to study the Book of Job, you will begin to notice the principle key to the book is God, in his sovereignty, revealing to Job what was in his heart – self-concern. When we let the Word of God get choked out due to the cares of this world, and Job had fears about things concerning his children, then we become unfruitful. Do you see this here Job was a righteous man, yet he did not take captive every thought to the obedience of Christ? You may be saying right about now, "I know you are crazy because Jesus wasn't even around yet." John 1:1 reveals the error in your question, "In the beginning was the Word, and the Word was with God, and the Word was God." Jesus is the Word; He has always been, and we have access to his presence through belief, repentance, his righteousness and his faith.

Job held a self-righteous attitude and concern that developed into a fear, and apparently, this is what Satan recognized, thus, the reason he showed up before the presence of the Lord. Satan was working on the fears that Job made available when he thought about his children and their relationship with God. Yes, of course, we are to care about our children, praying for them, directing them in the Word of God but we are not to fear. Give them to God, continue praying and speaking the Word but know God has them. Who are we to doubt God, and what he will do with his creation. Remember he formed them in their Mother's womb.

Job gave the devil a place to function in producing an opportunity to make Job unfruitful. When not bearing fruit, you are not experiencing peace. Even Job spoke it himself in 3:26, "I wasn't at ease, I wasn't quiet, I wasn't at rest." (Paraphrased). As long as you strive with a fear or concern, you are not going to find peace easily attainable. Look at yourself. Are you at odds with someone? Forgive them, simply forgive them. Give the matter over to God and trust him to deal with it in his way, not yours. Don't give the devil a place to work in your life. Don't let your religion become self-righteous - full of self-justifications and judgements of others.

At the end of Job's story, God shows up in the light of his almighty sovereignty. Are we sure we want to get to that point in our self-justification where we are faced with that almighty greatness? Job relents and sees himself in that light - the light that demands an answer of accountability before the very God that created him and breathed his Spirit into him. Job realizes no thought is withheld from this God of light (Job 42:2).

It is not my righteousness but his. It is not my self-sufficiency, but the will of him who sent me. It is the righteousness of Christ Jesus, our Savior. This humbling is the preparation of the soil of the heart that lets the seeds of peace sown grow and produce the fruit of peace in our lives. The true path to humility is a disciplined thought life guided by the Word and the Spirit of God.

Job repents and then God has Job incorporate the forgiveness given him by giving his friends up in prayer letting God do what he is

Sovereign over - forgiveness and love, peace and plenty.[34] [35] Seeds sown in peace produce righteousness (James 3:18). You must understand this peace is God's wholeness. It is His Holy Spirit. It is good. It is right. It is beautiful. It is acceptable. It is His Word. It is a prosperous way because Jesus was led of the Holy Spirit, never being caught in a conflict that cost him his peace. (Ephesians 2:14). Do not limit prosperity to financial success. When Satan uses those who oppress, giving them rule over us, they are usually the ones with a concept or sense of what, in this world's eyes, may be considered gain. They accomplish some position or achieve some authority and make some money on the way while believing themselves to be something. They place others beneath

---

[34] Do you pray? How do you pray? Job did not pray for his friends, who were judging him based on what they saw and how they felt about things while he was busy justifying himself. Job's fears were based on his opinions and judgements of his children. Are your fears found here? Do you leave your opinions of family, politics, work and friends as what dictates what is being said? When we speak or pray anything less then what is acceptable to the Most High God, then we are rebelling. This is why Satan could recognize Job's flaw because Satan is the master rebel. He recognized his own work being accomplished in Job. Job prayed with effect when he prayed in humility in the light of God's Sovereignty.

[35] This repentance is multifaceted because it involves (1) taking captive that thought that deceives. The thought that distracts or weighs us down with concern. Ask yourself what are the things that concern you, what causes a fear to develop that may, over time, distract and weigh on you sometimes to the point of consuming your thoughts which may lead to actions that you might regret? (2) Cast your care! Sometimes thoughts that enter your mind come with a strong push, a force that can be overwhelming; however, the immediate capture of that thought now needs an action that will contend with it. That action is the casting of that thought to the one who is able to absolve it of any worth. The force required is considered in Bible times to be an aggressive move taken at spear point. It either submits to your action, or you will run it through at spear point by using the Word of God powered by the fruit of the Holy Spirit. Stop taking the cares of this world, which are God's concern. (3) Humble yourself. Never let it be about you. Your flesh-sin nature is completely unable to grasp the power of the fruit of the Holy Spirit. It is only able to function to the level that a soul separated from God may operate in. As you humble yourself (which is not seeking dependence upon your own concepts, strengths, experiences, desires and emotions), and begin to repent of the thoughts and actions, you have done by taking captive your thoughts and casting those cares on the Sovereign God, then you will see your faith grow, your trust blossom, and your love for God plunge its roots deep into the soil of the Holy Spirit.

themselves to justify their own selfish ambition. Our understanding of prosperity is driven by the concepts we formulate based on what we take from our experience in this world system. Prosperity given by God is a result of peace, the peace of God. Peace is a wholeness that incorporates health, wealth, faith, right thinking, rest, fulfilling hope, the whole of his love and a life of trust in God that says we know we are his, and we shall not be moved. We gain understanding that what is here in this life on this earth is temporary and what we do have is a heavenly home in the presence of his peace.

So here we are learning that peace is an absence of conflict. That Satan uses conflict to bring division. That peace is irrevocably connected to sowing seed, being the fruit of the Holy Spirit, that Jesus gave us his share of peace by giving us the Holy Ghost and that is God's peace. The final question to answer here in this chapter is how do we obtain this peace? Throughout this book, we have referenced the love of God as it pertains to the different aspects of our life in relationship with a Holy God, a Creator God, a God of wisdom and might. But now we, in seeking a life of peace, must come to know just what this peace is truly rooted in. It is his love. This is what peace is.

Ephesians 3:19 reads, "And to know the love of Christ, which passes knowledge, that you might be filled with all the fulness of God."

Colossians 3:14-15 reads, "And above all these things put on love, which is the perfect bond of unity. And let the peace of God rule in your hearts …"

Philippians 4:7 reads, "And the peace of God, which passes all understanding, shall keep your hearts and minds through Christ Jesus."

Isaiah 26:3 reads, "Thou wilt keep him in perfect peace, whose mind is stayed on thee: because he trusts in thee."

I John 3:1 reads, "Behold what manner of love the Father has bestowed upon us, that we should be called the sons of God …"

I John 4:10 reads, "Herein is love, not that we loved God, but that he loved us, and sent his Son to be the propitiation for our sins."

I John 4:16 reads, "And we have known and believed the love that God has to us, God is love; and he that dwells in love dwells in God, and God in him."

Deuteronomy 6:5 reads, "And thou shalt love the Lord thy God with all thine heart, and with all thy soul, and with all thy might."

Psalm 18:1 reads, "I will love thee, O Lord, my strength."

Proverbs 10:12 reads, "Hatred stirs up strifes: but love covers all sins."

Song of Solomon 8:6,7 reads, "… for love is strong as death; jealousy is cruel as the grave… Many waters cannot quench love, neither can the floods drown it: if a man would give all the substance of his house for love, it would be utterly contemned."

Romans 8:35 reads, "Who shall separate us from the love of Christ? Shall tribulation, or distress, or persecution, or famine, or nakedness, or peril, or sword?"

God's love is bound by no man, yet it is given freely to all. It is ours to take. We have the choice to take this love. We are not bound by anything in making this choice except when we do not capture our thoughts to the obedience of Christ, and through this lack of obedience, we give place to the devil by yielding to thoughts that lead to offenses, anger, jealousies, bondages, and self-satisfactions. It is completely up to each of us as individuals. There is no one else to blame for which way we decide to go.

Hebrews 3:8 reads, "Harden not your hearts …"

Hebrews 3:12 reads, "Take Heed brethren, lest there be in any of you an evil heart of unbelief, in departing from the living God."

Hebrews 3:18 reads, "And to whom swear he that they should not enter into his rest, but to them that believed not."

Hebrews 4:3 reads, "For we which have believed do enter into rest ..."

If we intend to take the fullness of peace, we must believe that God is love and, in absolute certainty, we know that his love will, can, and does abide in us. If we stumble, if we make a mistake, if we resort back to an addiction, a failure, a hurt, or an anger, do not let the thief, who is a liar, deceive you into thinking you can no longer go on. You can't take any more of this. No, instead, look at that love that he alone can give. Don't look at the shortcomings, or setbacks as the ultimate outcome. Look at them as the opportunity, given by his sovereignty, to see what was in our heart that obstructs the true peace. Look at the insecurities that have developed in you, the pride that covers those insecurities. Most of all, look at how God's love is more than able to deliver and heal our brokenness. How it strengthens our character, our resolve, and how it gives us understanding in the circumstances and events of this life.

In I Corinthians 13, we find the chapter that gives us the explanation of love, and interestingly, the King James version of the Bible renders the word for love as charity. What do we do with a charity? We give to a charity so that the charity may give to those in need. In other words, charity may be described as a love that gives. We take of the fruit of the Spirit of love, and we are nourished. We take the seeds of love and sow them in peace. We give that love an opportunity to die to itself and grow again into an hundredfold, sixtyfold, and thirtyfold return. Love, God's love, always gives back.

If we confuse this love with our desires to be spent on how we satisfy ourselves, then we will produce hardness of heart over each time it doesn't fulfill, or falls short. You see, God's love does not contain selfishness. He doesn't give us what we think we need. He gives us what he knows is best for us, even during times of evil and conflict. Before we can love him we must first take his love through forgiveness because we can't truly love unselfishly in our sinful nature. This yielding, this humbling of ourselves to obtain that pure, perfect, unselfish love is the process the seed goes through when that hard outer shell is absolved into the tempers and pressures of the soil.

This is true love when you love through hardships and difficulties, angers and unwarranted hatred, gossip, and rumors. See how God is, even though we have been created by him in love, he does not stop being love when we disobey. He still loves us, even while we turn to our self, clinging to what we feel comfortable with. We want this comfort because we have troubles and fears, and we shrink away from them rather than face them. "My peace I give to you, let not your heart be troubled neither let it be afraid" says Jesus (John 14:27). "Jesus answered and said unto him, If a man love me, he will keep my words; and my Father will love him, and we will come unto him, and make our abode with him." (John 14:23). Whatever this world has to offer, when you come to believe, can, in no way, stop God himself, from dwelling in you in Spirit, touch him, listen to him, hold onto him for his love is in you.

Take a look at how his love is described in I Corinthians 13.

A giving love is patient. It is willing to suffer us a long time giving us time to grow up into love.

A giving love is kind. It doesn't return evil with evil. It expresses itself by doing good.

A giving love is not envious and does not produce jealousy, which is a lack of trust in our God that provides.

A giving love does not brag, or vaunt itself about itself, or places itself above anyone.

A giving love is not arrogant, or puffs itself up. It doesn't need to prove itself, or draw attention to itself.

A giving love does not act unbecomingly, or behave in an unseemly manner. In other words, it doesn't get stupid acting out foolishly to draw attention to itself.

A giving love does not seek her own. It is never about itself. Giving to yourself is rarely fulfilling.

A giving love is not provoked since it is never about satisfying itself. We become provoked when something doesn't go the way we think it should. Love doesn't think this way.

A giving love doesn't think evil. It doesn't take into account any thought that would leave it separated from God.

A giving love does not rejoice in iniquity, or that which is unjust, or what ought not to be may still happening.

A giving love rejoices, or sympathizes in gladness with truth, or honesty. Getting to the real root of any matter determines that, which is true, or that, which is false in appearance only by looking good on the outside but without true reality.

A giving love bears all things no matter if it be good you encounter in this life, or evil in the form of heartbreak, or hatred, or words slung at you with intent to hurt. Because it trusts and knows God is the judge of all.

A giving love believes all things that he directs our path, regardless of our decisions because it is the path that leads through love that he wants us to follow.

A giving love hopes all things. It is expectantly waiting for a known and expected end provided by God's promises.

A giving love endures all things. No matter the pain, or the suffering, love stays. It doesn't find the fault, or blame.

A giving love never fails, it doesn't fall away when temptations come, or conflicts arise. A giving love, God's love, is everlasting. If love were to fail, then God would fail, and the end of us would be beyond any horrific imagination we might think of.

The fruit of the Spirit is so intertwined with the love of God that they are the same. I may not have one without the other. When I am producing the fruit of the Spirit, I am presenting a harvest of love, which is God Himself. Do not be overwhelmed by this. Mark 4:26-27 tells us when the seed is sown by us, we than go about our daily lives sleeping and rising. While we are doing this, the seed springs up pushing its blade through the earth and diving its roots deeper into the soil gaining nutrients and moisture. We may scientifically explain this agricultural process today, but it still remains outside of our knowledge just exactly what is in that seed to cause it to do what it does. But it does it. When we plant the seeds of the fruit of the Spirit, we are doing our job of tending the garden. It is God's doing to send the rain, to put in that seed the desire, the will to succeed. So it grows, it endures the growing season, and in the end, produces a harvest.

We are in this, whether we think so or not. Whether we believe it or not. This is the principle set forth in the beginning by God the Creator when he planted the Garden. Our freedom is in the preparation of the soil. Our diligence is in the tending of that garden. Our reward is in the dying to self to gain a harvest. When we settle this in our hearts and minds that the things of this world are not the end for us, than we begin to reap a harvest of peace because we leave the things that we are not responsible for to the One who is Sovereign.

Luke 6:43-45 speaks of us not going to a thorn tree to pick figs, or a briar bush to pick grapes. While our freedom is the preparation of the soil, and God directs our path, we must tend to that heart and what it allows to grow. A good man out of the good treasure of his heart brings out good. Consequently, an evil man brings evil out of his heart for out of the abundance of the heart his mouth speaks (Luke 6:45). Peace is with the good man because he has treasured up in his heart those things that tend to love. The evil man will not come to peace and speaks the things of this world over the things of love. If you are the latter person, you don't have to be this way. Plough the soil of your heart to take in the seeds of love, peace, right and good. Ask God to give you a new heart, ask him to forgive you and you will see the weeds begin to wither.

Against Such Things there is No Law

One last point to deliver before we leave this chapter is this: When the principle of sowing and reaping was set forth by God in the beginning as he planted the garden, he then established that there is no law against the fruit of the Spirit. There is no restriction, no constriction, no regulation, no perimeter set that we must abide in. This is the beauty of this whole thing that there is no limit to how God moves in his love. No, he created everything in his love that is why, try as we might, we are, in this lifetime, not going to come to a comprehensible knowledge of the complexities of all that exists around us from the law of physics to the unseen realm of faith. We cannot study the human body enough to know everything about it. Nor will we study the stars enough to know all that vast expanse of the universe. Look at the amount of time we have lived on this earth, and we are still discovering amazing things about this planet. We will always be discovering, we will always be growing, and we will always be gaining knowledge of his Spirit and his love. Therefore, there is no law that dictates, or limits how much love you may show, or how much joy you may have, or how much peace you may live in, or how much patience to demonstrate, or how much kindness you may bestow, or how much goodness to do, or how much faithfulness to exercise, or how much gentleness to give towards someone, or how much self-control to be under in times of hardness and temptation (Galatians 5:22-23).

Let our hearts be given to the one who loves us, who is love, who created us in love. If you have a father, or mother here on earth that never gave you love, let it go. There is one who willingly gave his life, in love, because of love, and out of love for you. You will find peace here; the peace Jesus gave us through the Holy Spirit. The peace that passes all our understanding and all of our reasonings shall surely keep our *hearts* and *minds* through the Anointed One and his Anointing, the man, the Son of God, Jesus (Philippians 4:7).

Ephesians 3:17-19 reads, "That Christ may dwell in your hearts by faith; that you being rooted and grounded in love, May be able to comprehend with all saints what is the breadth, and length, and depth, and height: And to know the love of Christ, which passes knowledge, that you might be filled with all the fullness of God."

This peace we all desire is not about what we accomplish, or what awards we may gain, or what pleasures we would like to see fulfilled. It is not about the process of dying to self with the hardness of those circumstances and difficulties and what we think this may cost us. It is about gaining Christ. It is about Christ dwelling within us. Are we even able to comprehend this? Yes, we are! We are able to embrace within the limits of our flesh the broad scope of the love of Christ, even though it passes knowledge, you are able to discover a filling of all the fullness of God. If this were not possible, than God would be a fake. But *with* God all things are possible (Mark 10:27). Live in his love and you will reap his peace.

CHAPTER 7

GIVE THANKS

To Give Thanks; is a demonstration of gratitude towards a benefit bestowed upon
Or performed to your own personal benefit or the benefit of Another.

Here we are at the last chapter of this book in which we have seen the give and take in our salvation, in our respect for each other, in our offenses and our forgiveness, in our hope, in our love and in our faith. We have seen what has been given to us for use as weapons and how we are to take captive our thoughts. We acknowledge how the Holy Spirit has been given to us for comfort, truth and in fruit bearing to bring us a peace that simply passes all of our earthly understanding. Now we come to giving thanks. How telling is this about us?

Are we able to truly give thanks during our most hard moments? Do we give thanks that is truly heartfelt, or is it shallow used just as a common response while in a distant conversation? Do we give thanks to our Father, our Creator? He knows how things grow. He designed them. He knows you. He knows where you have been, what you are doing, and where you are going. He knows what you need to hear to prick your heart, to prune you, whether it is in tragedy or triumph. At every crossroad, at every event, at every turning point, he is there. You may choose him, or you may choose you. If you choose him, then giving thanks for his sovereignty, his love and mercy, his protection and deliverance will become a very real and important part of your life. It will change who you are. It will change how others perceive you. It will change how you accept this life you are born into. So let's see what the Spirit of God has to teach us on giving thanks.

Simple Truths

To give is to render something to someone from that, which you have. You cannot give what you do not have. You do not give a gift to someone if you do not have a gift to give. Giving is when you are not concerned about holding onto something. If you want to hold onto that offense, then you cannot give forgiveness (Matthew 6:14-15). If you don't have thankfulness in your heart, you will not have it to give. If you have a complaint in your heart, than you cannot give out thankfulness to the one you love.

Right about now, you are telling me, "I don't have a heart that is willing to forgive. I don't have thankfulness in my heart. How can I when that person continually does stupid, mean, and hurtful things to me. God just can't use me because I just can't be thankful." Well you're right. As long as you choose to be ungrateful, unforgiving, and unrepentant, you can't be thankful with a heart full of unforgiveness and complaining. But know where this kind of condemnation comes from. It is either your self-sin nature, or Satan. God is not in the business of condemnation. He is in the business of healing the broken hearted. Condemnation is a self-judgement presented by you, or someone else with a condemning attitude. Conviction is a work of the Holy Spirit. To be convicted by the Holy Spirit is a pointing out of what you need changed in your life, your character, and your personality. You may work with God by simply asking him to give you a thankful heart, and He will begin the process of revealing that one thing you lack.

In Matthew 19, a young man with riches came to Jesus and asked, "What good thing shall I do that I may have eternal life?" Jesus answers to obey the commandments of Moses and come follow him, and the young man said, "I have kept all of these from my youth until now." Jesus points out that one thing that is keeping the young man from obtaining what he desired, that one thing that prevents him from entering that life that is wholly the Lords. Jesus says, "Go and sell what you have and give to the poor." When the young man hears these words, he knew he was faced with a choice to give up his riches and give to the poor, or walk away keeping what he had. One choice will lead to trust and faith, to learning his precepts, to knowing him, walking with him, loving him, and being loved by him, we should remember the principle of sowing and reaping. Seed does not grow if you hold onto it, it must be broadcast, or planted. Holding onto what you have means you are not willing to give. When you are willing to give, in love, you can expect a harvest to come in due season. Look at the treasure that would have been available to the rich young man had he given what he had. Seeing the hand of God provide a defense for you, to give you provision because you trusted him. The other choice will take you no further than you already are. Your reward is already in your hand. This is all you will ever have. But if you give what you have, that part of your "self" that needs to go before he can trust you with his filling, you will grow in faith, in peace, in mercy, in grace, in his love. You will bear fruit because it is not of you doing the work to fulfill yourself, but his doing.

The young man went away sorrowful because he hung onto his "self". His desires toward his riches were greater than his desire to gain eternal life. Giving to the poor is exactly what God the Father does for us. This giving up of our-selves to a loving, faithful, and true God surely brings with it a heart that desires to express thankfulness. Now we need to express that thankfulness towards God and others by doing his Word. Colossians 1:12 reads, "Giving thanks unto the Father, which hath made us to be the partakers of the inheritance of the saints in light." Colossians 3:17 reads, "And whatever you do in word or deed, do all in the name of the Lord Jesus, giving thanks to God and the Father by him." Continual thoughts, attitudes, and actions of giving thanks is giving praise to God, honoring God, and blessing God. It is recognizing he is sovereign, he is above all, and he is the Creator. Psalm 100:3-4 reads, "Know ye that the Lord he is God: it is he that has made us, not we ourselves; we are his people, and the sheep of his pasture. Enter into his gates with thanksgiving and into his courts with praise: be thankful unto him, and bless his name," hanging onto what we have materially and emotionally, will only derail us from his eternal blessings which are ours in inheritance.

By giving thanks, we, with our thoughts, attitudes and actions are becoming obedient which is greater to God than any sacrifice we may offer in our own deceits. (1 Samuel 15:22) Obedience comes with equal parts of submitting humbly before God and giving thanks for all he is, for all he gives us and for all his tender loving kindnesses. Ephesians 5:1-4 reads, "Be ye therefore followers of God as dear children: And walk in love, as Christ also has loved us, and has *given* himself for us an offering and a sacrifice to God for a sweet-smelling savor. But fornication, and all uncleanness, or covetousness, let it not be once named among you, as becomes saints; Neither filthiness, nor foolish talking, nor jesting, which are not convenient: *but rather giving of thanks.*" (italics added). Psalm 119:62 tells us that when we rise at midnight, we are to give thanks because of His righteous judgements. In giving thanks, I am rendering my acknowledgement that I depend on him, no longer being concerned about my self-satisfaction but doing his pleasure.

In the Old Testament, the word used for thanks is *yadah,* which, according to Strong's 3034 the definition, is "to throw, to cast, to speak out, to confess; to praise, to sing, to give thanks, to thank." It is the root of the name Judah who was one of the sons of Jacob making him one of the twelve tribes of Israel of which tribe Jesus was descended from. The significance of throwing, or casting, or speaking out to our Father in heaven those things, which so easily beset us, is evident through our confession in a manner that causes us to sing, to praise, to give thanks. We are not to be in drudgery to our sins or setbacks. It is not our circumstances that dictate our attitude and response. By praise and thanksgiving with a joyful noise, we are lifted up above these petty things.

Sorrow has no place in giving. Joyful giving with the giving of thanks brings blessing. If the young man who was rich would have had a heart of thanks towards God for what God had given him, he would have joyfully given what he had to the poor and would have had unimaginable treasure in heaven. You can see the result of his decision. It wasn't joy. He went away from the Lord Jesus in sorrow. What did he actually give up here? A chance to follow Jesus. Read back through this story and reference the same story in Mark 10 and see where Jesus answers the young man but pay special attention to the point in verse 21 that Mark makes where Jesus looked at him and loved him. The Lord knew what this man had done in his life, and he knew what was holding the young man back, and He spoke directly to it in love. It is not the wealth the man had that held him at bay from following the Lord with his whole heart it was the fact he was unwilling to give it up. The sorrow the young man had demonstrated that he knew what his choice was and what it would cost him. Had he chosen to give, it would have been easy to come and follow Jesus because it would have no longer been about him trying to gain by works, it would have been about Jesus.

We must understand every time we sin and every time we take captive a thought whose goal is to deceive us, and we give it over to the Lord, we are set free from this bondage. This is where giving thanks with singing and joy raises us to a realm that falls under the shadow of his wings. That's a closeness, a resting, an assurance that we, in all our self-consciousness, cannot attain through the devices that this world offers (Ephesians2:4-5).

The Will of God

I Thessalonians 5:18 reads, "In everything give thanks: for this is the will of God in Christ Jesus concerning you." Are we aware of this? How many times have we wondered what the will of God is for our lives? How often have we gotten mad at God for allowing this adversity that is upon us? This can't be the will of God we may reason. Why would a God allow this kind of evil to happen? Maybe you are a Christian already, and you are all fired up to serve and live for the Lord, but you don't know what he wants you to do, or how to do it. These are questions often kicked around by many of us at varying points in our lives. The will of God is much easier to ascertain when we see with the eyes of our spirit and not the eyes of our flesh (Galatians 5:16; Romans 8:1, 4-8).

Doing the will of God starts with salvation, then moves to respect for others and yourself. When you get to the point where you do not take offense and are quick to forgive and to ask for forgiveness, you are doing the will of God. As you live your life in hope of his promises by love and by faith, you are doing the will of God. When you use the weapons of warfare by taking captive every thought to the obedience of Christ, you are doing the will of God. When you take the peace that Christ left us through his Holy Spirit, you are doing the will of God. When you give thanks for his everyday mercy and love, you are doing the will of God. Follow this path, and you will find it far more reliable in knowing what he wants you to do rather than chasing an idea that may have been born out of your flesh. Always trust Him with the answer.

We will take a look at three examples of people - Daniel, David, and the Apostle John - who gave thanks shedding some light on this subject and possibly giving an answer to our questions. Each of these men lived in different times in history experiencing the moments of conflict, the exaltations, the heartbreaks, and the sovereignty of the God many of us have complained about with many of their circumstances being far more difficult then what most of us have ever experienced in our lives.

Daniel

Daniel was born into a time when Israel had come to the resulting consequences and end of its compromising and rebellious attitude toward God. In chapter 1 verse 2 of the book of Daniel, we will find where God gave the King of Israel into the hand of Nebuchadnezzar, the King of Babylon. The time had come for Israel to be confronted and held accountable for its rebellious attitude to God, so he gave them over to captivity.[36] Captivity and bondage are a part of this world. God absolutely knows how to accomplish his Word through this path: regardless of how we may perceive him. Evil, on the other hand, seeks to bring you into captivity and bind you from your freedoms in Christ. God is never held back by these things. Our God rules over them. See his Sovereignty at work here by establishing the Babylonian Empire to cause Israel to endure captivity to bring them to obedience.

Look at Ephesians 4:7-10 where Jesus, upon his death on the cross, descended to the grave and laying hold of captivity he led it as a captive itself and took the spoils of his victory and distributes them as gifts to men. The sovereignty of this is found in Ephesians 4:4-6 where all of this is clearly set forth. There is one body. There is one Spirit. There is one Hope. There is one Lord. There is one faith. There is one baptism.

---

[36] God knows the outcome of all the options we may be faced with, and it is our choice that determines, which option we will take. God gives us opportunity to know him, learn of him, trust him and hope in him at every decision we contemplate daily. If we choose a path that distracts or deceives or is self-serving, he will always be ready to accept a repentant heart. He is willing to allow us to make wrong choices that sometimes lead to difficult lives and hardships, and he will give us over to these paths as long as we have a hardened heart unwilling to turn to him. Know this that we have the choice right now to turn to him in trust and faith before a hardship comes along. Should the hardship, through his mercy, be averted or whether it happens: we will be at rest and peace by choosing to know him as our deliverer.

There is one God who is the Father of us all, who is above all, who is through all and in all of us. This plan has been from the beginning of the foundations of the earth. Think about it. No one ever built a house without first having a design, a set of plans to construct it with. Do you really think God is shooting from the hip, making this up as he goes? Jesus paid the price so that all things - bondages and captivities included - would be put under his feet.

Back to Daniel. We find a young boy whose whole world is being turned upside down. Being taken captive and hauled off to a foreign land with a strange language. Daniel and three of his relatives came from the tribe of Judah as princes interesting that they came from the tribe whose root meaning is giving thanks and praise. More interesting is they are the ones of all the sons of Israel that stood in faithfulness and gave thanks to God. How is this? Take a look at Daniel 1:8 in the King James version where it states it this way, "But Daniel purposed in his heart..." The New American Standard Bible reads this way, "But Daniel made up his mind ..." Despite the events that led them to this point with the Babylonian army conquering Jerusalem and the land of Israel, watching others around them being killed and having been taken from their homes being forced into service of a foreign people, Daniel exacted in his heart and mind that he would remain faithful to the one true God of Israel.

Apply this to today's times. Are there not multitudes around this world moving to a foreign country, some on their own volition, some having to do so without choice, and some as the only possible way for the safety of their families' lives? Look at our own lives how we are held in bondage to controlling, hurtful, manipulating people, or circumstances. How are you handling it? Is it overwhelming you, or placing stress upon your life? Are you looking at it as though there is no way out? Does it bring fear with it? Daniel handled it with a mind that was settled. He purposed in his heart that he would remain faithful and give thanks. This led to a complete trust that God was sovereign, even amongst these conditions that surrounded him. This brought him into a favor that God was willing to give. Opening up an opportunity that brought a promotion to being second in command over an empire. You may not be promoted to running a nation, but through Christ and faithfulness in him, you will be promoted over your circumstances. The circumstances that Daniel had been forced into did not go away. He still remained in captivity, but living in those circumstances just got a whole lot better for him and all the Israelites. Instead of being under those circumstances he now ruled over them with a thankful heart. Every moment we spend complaining, we are placing ourselves deeper under our circumstances. Every moment we give thanks and praise from a settled heart and mind, we gain his love and favor, his mercy and grace, with a bountiful hope.

Because Daniel and his three relatives were faithful and ate the food God instructed Israel to eat, so as to obtain a healthy body, they were given by God knowledge and skill in learning, wisdom, and understanding, which led to an opportunity (Daniel 1:17). The King of the Babylonian Empire had a dream. He was perplexed by this dream to the point he was losing sleep over it. The king is thinking, *I have all of these magicians, conjurers, sorcerers and Chaldean soothsayer priests to tell me what the dream was and give me the interpretation of it.* They are summoned to come before the king to hear his request. When they heard what he wanted they responded, "… tell us the dream and we will show the interpretation." (Daniel 2:4). Here comes the problem to their response. The king couldn't remember the dream. Have you ever dreamed a dream, and the next morning, you knew you had a dream but couldn't remember the dream? Well, such is the case here. The people who the king relied upon to bring knowledge to him were selling him short on knowledge. The king decided if they could not give the king the dream *and* the interpretation, than they might as well be, all of them, cut into pieces and their homes made into manure piles. Ouch! The pressure is on for these guys. They did not perform well under this pressure because their response was, "There is not a man upon the earth that can show the King's matter." (Daniel 2:10).

As you might expect, this really fired up the King. In furious anger, he commanded all the wise men of Babylon be destroyed. This included all the learned and knowledgeable as well Daniel and his three relatives from Judah. This news comes to Daniel, and he asks the guy who the King put in charge of the execution of all these people what the reason for this was. When he hears the reason for the king's command, he goes straight into the king and asks for time to show the interpretation to the king. Daniel goes back to the house and gets with his relatives, Han-a-niah, Misha-el, and Az-a-riah (whom you may recognize as Shadrach, Meshach and A-bed-ne-go) and call on the mercies of God concerning this secret. Something to note here is that God will not reveal his mysteries to those who choose not to believe, but he will to those who are faithful (Psalm 25:14). This is why the wise men of Babylon were unable to render an interpretation.

That night, God revealed to Daniel in a vision the secret of the King's dream. What was Daniel's response at this moment of time that demands an action? Either bring an interpretation to the king, or a whole lot of people were about to be dismembered. This is looking death right in the eyes and not flinching. Once again, how did Daniel handle this? By blessing the name of God for ever and ever and by giving thanks and praise. Daniel 2:20 and 23 reads, "Daniel answered and said, Blessed be the name of God for ever and ever: for wisdom and might are his: I thank thee, and praise thee, O thou God of my fathers, who hast given me wisdom and might, and hast made known unto me now what we desired of thee: for thou has now made known unto us the King's matter."

When you are in those difficult times that demand an action, how do you handle it? Do you resort back to fear (which paralyzes action), or do you fall on the mercies of the one true God? Ask him for the knowledge and wisdom to discern the action to take with the first action being that of giving thanks. When you give thanks to God first, when you praise him and have coming out of your heart this

146

acknowledgement that he is sovereign and the results are in his hands, then you are above your circumstances.

Daniel delivers the dream and the interpretation to King Nebuchadnezzar. No one else was able to, and even Daniel doesn't take credit for it. He even said, "But as for me, this secret is not revealed to me for any wisdom that I have more than any living person." (Daniel 2:30). Daniel doesn't claim he is wiser or better than anyone else. Instead, he gives all the credit to God. This is knowing the position we are in with the sovereign God. Understanding that we are because he alone is, and there is no other God. He was confident in this. He was at rest with this. This gave him a spirit that was at peace. This is why he was known as a man with an "excellent spirit".

When you have this understanding and knowledge of the Most High God, then you will find it easy to give thanks to him. Why? Because you know everything you have comes from him. To those who have much and those who have little, if you were to gain this understanding, then what you do have will become more valuable, especially when you begin giving him thanks for what you do have.

Remember we looked at 1 Thessalonians 5:18 and saw that giving thanks is the will of God, and as we see in this example of Daniel that he gives thanks for the wisdom given to him by God. Being in the will of God is far simpler than we tend to make it at times. When you give love like Christ gave love for us, you are in the will of God. As you become grateful and give thanks to him for who he is, you are in the will of God. He knows who you are. He knows how you are made. His Son endured shame, deceit, betrayal, hatred, physical abuse, critical thinking, and wrong opinions from others. There is nothing you have been touched with that he does not understand. You see the two go hand in hand. We give out thanks to God and he is willing to give out wisdom.

Bear in mind that Daniel had earlier been faced with a decision that could easily have cost him his life. He purposely chose to obey God in what he was to eat. Daniel did not compromise the instruction of the Lord. He stayed faithful. Take time to study for yourself the things God loves and promises and the things he hates, you might discover why it behooves us to obey and remain faithful. Look at all the daily unfolding of our lives and how the world has force fed us compromise. Who are you trying to fool? Your own-self? God? Maybe your wife, or husband, or friends, or boss, or authorities, but who are you really trying to fool? You cannot have a truth while sprinkling compromise on it and expect a quality outcome. When you stay faithful, you are getting wiser because you are seeing things through his sovereign eyes. Do you hear the truth and turn it to fit your decisions so you may feel better about what you are doing? Do you come to accept things the world is offering because you don't want to face the possible outcome the world's standards have set. If you are compromising because of fear, then don't expect God to deliver wisdom to you.

Wisdom comes to people in many varying ways. It was given by God as a skill for those who were chosen to build the Temple under Moses. For Daniel, it came as discretion and discernment, counsel, and wisdom in handling the captain of the King's guard while he was rounding up the wise and knowledgeable to be executed (Daniel2:14). You can't be discerning and calm while reacting in fear and panic. Daniel did what he had to do by seeking time from the king so he and those who were obedient with him could turn to the Lord and hear from him.

Take a look at Psalm 111. It begins with praise and giving of thanks with our whole heart, and it ends with the fear of the Lord as the beginning of wisdom. Wisdom is everywhere in the Bible, but we cannot see it with our natural eyes. We must see it by the Spirit of God. Job speaks of it in chapter 28 of his story. David speaks of it throughout the Psalms. The book of Proverbs desires us to seek it out. But we are blind to it because we don't fear the Lord. Luke 12:4-5 tells us to not fear man who is able to kill us, and after that, they can do nothing else to us. Instead, we are to fear the one who, after we have been killed, has authority to cast us into hell. When we begin to see ourselves as one who is created and stop looking at our lives as though we are the ones who created ourselves, than we may begin to open the eyes of our understanding to see him as the purest form of love there is. This is coming to fear the Lord, this is the beginning of wisdom (Psalm 111:10; Proverbs 9:10).

When Daniel was taken away into the captivity as a young boy, the King of Judah was Je-hoia-kim. At this time, the prophet Jeremiah was still alive. The word that Jeremiah was giving the Nation of Israel was not a kind and peaceful word. It was a word of judgement coming upon Israel that if they do not turn from the rebellious attitude they had acquired against the God of Israel, they would be conquered and taken into captivity. While Jeremiah is preaching that captivity is upon the nation, the religious leaders and the king, eventually send him to prison. This word from the Lord that Jeremiah spoke, the imprisonment, and the fulfilling of the Word, was the news of the land. Everyone in Israel and Judah heard of the prophet Jeremiah and what he spoke. This means Daniel, even as a young boy, when he would attend the synagogue, in all probability, heard these prophesies. Now fast forward to Daniel chapter 9, we see Daniel praying for and confessing the sins of his people. Verse 13 attributes what is written in the law of Moses how the rebelliousness and sin are the reason the evil of the captivity came upon Israel. That the Israelites would not pray to God and turn their hearts toward Him.

Daniel was obviously impacted by the word of the prophet watching it unfold before his very eyes. Making the decision to remain faithful to God and knowing him as the sovereign Most High God was certainly influenced by the events of the fall of Jerusalem and the fulfillment of prophesy spoken by Jeremiah. So he prays for the sins of his people. Not only was Daniel faithful, but now he is confessing through prayer to God the sins of the people. What happens next for Daniel is a moment that has transcended history itself. While he is still praying the angel Gabriel, who was sent swiftly to Daniel, touched him, and began to inform him of future events by giving him skill, insight and understanding.

149

This wisdom, this skill, this understanding that come from God is given to those who ask (James 1:5), who remain faithful (Hebrews 10:22-23) and who confess their sins to him (1 John 1:9). Confession keeps us in right standing in our relationship with him. It shows God that we desire to remain dependent upon him for the fulfilling of his promises, that we fear and revere him and for his deliverance from evil. Because wisdom is a knowing that he has always been, that being rightly related to him removes us from the realm of fear (1 John 4:18). When we do not fear man, we are able to stand in adversity as Jeremiah did when being faced with angry people who wanted him to shut up threatening to kill him. As Moses who stood before mighty Pharaoh. As David who stood before a violent, threatening giant of a man named Goliath. As Elijah who stood before a king and all the people of the land calling down fire consuming the sacrifice, the wood, the water, and the dust. We look at this world and let it dictate our outcome, but looking to Jesus, and knowing his love and authority gives us wisdom to combat the world.

Yes, Daniel, by giving thanks, kept a heart that stayed true to the God who lives. He was doing the will of God in the process. It wasn't the circumstances that dictated his giving of thanks. It was his right relationship with a holy God who desires to give wisdom liberally. Through his faithfulness and peaceful spirit, Daniel was able to reap the fruit of the Holy Spirit, in his actions of doing he was given wisdom and understanding.

Take Time to Study

Study these scriptures on wisdom.

James 3:13-18 speaks of how a wise man shows it (wisdom) by the way he speaks and behaves. He isn't wild but controlled. If your intentions are based on bitter jealousy, envying, strife, and selfish ambition than what you think is wisdom really isn't wisdom at all. Check your intentions, what is in your heart, is it self-promoting, self-protecting, judgmental over others? This wisdom is not from above, but it is earthly, sensual, devilish. Earthly wisdom is from this world system of which Satan is the god of. Sensual wisdom is from the natural sinful man which is unable to assimilate the wisdom of God because sin has separated it from God. Devilish wisdom comes from demonic influence upon our thoughts and bodies. Bringing with it hatred, self-will, judgmental evil thoughts, and division along with sickness, sorrow, and self-pity.

1 Corinthians 3:17-20 speaks about how the wisdom of this world system is foolishness with God. He knows the thoughts of the wise of this world that they are vain and useless because they do not include God. Thoughts of wisdom that do not include God are shallow, empty and have no eternal value whatsoever.

1 Corinthians 1:18-20; 2:1-16 speaks that the worlds wisdom does not lead us to know God because we have turned to our own thinking thereby rejecting the wisdom of God. In so doing, by our reliance on our own thoughts, God left us to ourselves. God is willing to let us choose to believe and remain faithful or harden our hearts towards the Savior. Without faith it is foolish thinking to believe that a God would give up his Son to be a part of humanity, suffer in that fleshly body, die on a humiliating cross, and rise again from the dead to give life to anyone who chooses to believe and take this free salvation. This kind of wisdom is not attainable in the flesh but is absolutely a work of the Holy Spirit of God. Reference the above verses in 1 Corinthians chapters 1 & 2 with Romans 1:18-32 and 2:1-5 where Paul explains to us that when God made us, he put the evidence of himself within us. We don't have an excuse to not know him. So the strong desires in our heart are there because God, in is infinite wisdom and love, gave us the right to choose life, or choose death. When you follow, on this earth, a life that gives good, love, mercy, peace, hope, blessing, and kindness, than you are doing the will of God - knowing him.

151

When you exchange the truth of God for a lie to your own self-gratification, than you no longer see fit to acknowledge God. This is why everyday of rejection leads us deeper into wickedness, greed, evil, envy, murder, strife, deceit, malice, gossips, slanders, hatred of God and each other. Continuing on as insolent, arrogant, boastful, inventors of evil, disobedient to parents, without understanding, untrustworthy, unloving, unmerciful and on a path to death (Cf Galatians 5:19-21; Titus 3:3-5).

Isaiah 29:13-16, Job 28:1-28, along with Proverbs chapters 8 & 9 tells us prudence, knowledge and discretion exist with wisdom. Hating evil, which is anything not dependent on God, is the fear of the Lord. This is where you begin the path to wisdom by loving what he loves and hating what he hates. This is where Daniel set himself apart because he loved God by remaining obedient and continually seeking God for his wisdom which empowers us to accomplish God's will.

David

Our next example of giving thanks will be David, a shepherd boy who became king. First, let's do a lead up of what transpired in Israel before we get into this man that a large portion of the Old Testament is written about.

There was a time when Israel had no earthly king, but the God of Israel was their King. God did reign over His people. Many a time after sinning, Israel did watch and witness the deliverance from the countries that would rise up against them when they would repent and call upon God. Nevertheless, Israel decided they wanted the prophet Samuel to appoint an earthly king over them. Samuel saw this as an evil thing, but God told him in I Samuel 8:7 that the people were not rejecting Samuel, for he had been judging Israel from his youth to his old age, but they were, in fact, rejecting God himself. While it was Samuel who judged the people during his life, it was still God that Samuel received his direction from.

Samuel spoke to the people in chapter 12 reminding them of what the past had been for them, but in verse 12, he puts it to them bluntly by repeating their rejection of the Lord to their ears, "Nay: but a king shall reign over us." Thereby, specifying what the people wanted. They had made a decision to set aside the Lord their God as their King. The importance of this decision is still with us today. The Lord our God, Creator of heaven and earth, is our king if we so choose to yield to this. Earthly kings take from us to satisfy the government of their rule (1 Samuel 8:10-22). God, in his reign over us, gives to us more than we know, or understand (Deuteronomy 28:1-14). When you expect the government of the king to supply your protection and needs, you are, in reality, rejecting the rule of the Most High God. No government on this earth can bring the rain, nor make the seed grow. It cannot stop the wind, or cause the earth to tremble. The one true God holds this in his hand. If he is able to hold the waters by his command, than he is able to hold us.

God tells Samuel to listen to the people and anoint them a king. Following God's instructions, Samuel takes a man named Saul from the tribe of Benjamin. In 1 Samuel 10:1, Samuel took a vial of oil and poured it upon the head of Saul to demonstrate the work of the Holy Spirit upon a ruler. Israel had themselves a king. A difference to be noted here is Saul was anointed to be king with a vial of oil (1 Samuel 10:1), but when David was anointed, God told Samuel to fill his horn with oil (1 Samuel 16:1). There is a difference in anointing, but we must bear in mind it is still an anointing. Saul was anointed with enough to remain obedient and rule the people if he so chose.

Saul became king, and after all the hoopla was over, he simply went home. Well, it wasn't long before events occurred that pressed Saul into service. 1 Samuel 11, he has to confront the Ammonite people and defeats them. Next came the conflict with the Philistines who sorely outnumbered Israel (1 Samuel 13:5). What happens when you look at things, and it looks overwhelming? What do you do? The Israelites who had been in conflict with the Philistines for a long time had no weaponry because the Philistines would not allow a blacksmith for fear the Israelites might fabricate swords (1 Samuel 13:19-20). Because of this oppression and control the Israelites were under, they were focused on the wrong thing. They wanted a King but did not trust him to bring deliverance against overwhelming odds. They were not relying on God to bring deliverance because they were reacting in fear. Look how fear makes us act, some of them went and hid themselves. Some ran the other way and crossed over the Jordan River, but no matter how they responded, they were all distressed due to the circumstances. Distress does not breed courage. Running and hiding does not bring deliverance. Most certainly, none of them running and hiding were giving thanks for what this situation looked like.

Saul remained at home waiting for Samuel to come and give direction from God. Samuel didn't show up on the day they expected him; Saul, then, went ahead and made sacrifice to God without Samuel. What Saul did here is he went by what he saw. He did not involve faith and trust in God. He was not patient, resting in God to deliver. Samuel shows up just as soon as Saul had finished doing Samuel's job. Samuel poses that one question that always confronts us with a choice to repent, or make an excuse, "What have you done?" he asks (1 Samuel 13:6-12). The question here is why was Saul waiting at home in Gilgal? Saul had already been anointed to be king to perform the tasks of a king. Why was Samuel late in coming? When we are given a task from God to perform, and he supplies an anointing to go along with that task, then you have been empowered to accomplish what he has set before you. Sitting and waiting may not be the right recourse to follow. Doing something that someone else is anointed to do most likely will fail. Look at 1 Samuel 10:9. After Samuel had anointed Saul to be king and gave him instructions to follow, as soon as Saul turned to leave Samuel God instantly gave him another heart. This means that what was needed to be king was now placed in him. This is what grace does for us today - it empowers, it provides, it develops, and it holds us up with a new heart. Quit possibly, Samuel was late in coming because God wanted to test what was in Saul's heart.

Saul made an excuse. He chose poorly. This particular trial broke apart for him the moment the Philistines gathered themselves together to fight with Israel. Even though God had given him another heart, Saul, apparently, had not settled in his new heart the commands of the Lord, for he did not follow them. Had Saul remained obedient and rested in God despite what he saw (1 Samuel 13:11), he would have, at that moment, allowed the Lord to establish his kingdom upon Israel forever (1 Samuel 13:13). People look for leadership. If leadership acts in doubt, fear, and unbelief, or divisiveness, the people will follow that same concept. Saul's inaction to confront the overwhelming forces of the Philistines gave the people over to their fear. Saul's son Jonathan acted differently, and the outcome was supernatural at its finest. 1 Samuel 14:6 has Jonathan and his armor bearer alone go to the camp of the multitude of Philistines, and this is what he thought about this circumstance, "Come, let us go over unto the garrison of these uncircumcised: It may be that the Lord will work for us: for there is no restraint to the Lord to save by many or by few." The armor bearer's response shows the courage that is produced by leadership that is portrayed in confidence and authority knowing that it is God that saves and not we ourselves. 1 Samuel 14:7 "…Do all that is in thine heart: turn thee; behold, I am with thee according to thy heart." Courage overcomes fear when you no longer are concerned about your "self". Jonathan's action gave God the glory, and he brought deliverance from the Philistines. Just over two years into his service as King of Israel, Samuel informs Saul he acted foolishly and that the Lord has sought out a man after his own heart to replace him (1 Samuel 13:14). That man would end up being David.

Saul and Israel pervaded over the Philistines as well as enemies on every side in part by the courageous action of the faith of Jonathan (1 Samuel 16:47-48). There is one more incident that occurs with Saul as king that seals his fate and sets the stage for David to be king. 1 Samuel 15 has the Lord telling Saul through Samuel to utterly destroy all the Amalekites both men and women, babies, oxen, sheep, camels and donkeys. Everything must be destroyed. Before you go wondering why this God of love I have been writing about would want to destroy his own creation, you must remember he is also a God of judgement. When Israel was delivered from the bondage of Egypt, and they were traveling to the Promised land. The Amalekites came from the rear and attacked God's chosen people. They killed those who were feeble and those who were faint and weary. Amalek did not fear God, acting in cowardice by coming up from behind, killing the defenseless and the helpless (Exodus 17:8 and 14-16; Deuteronomy 25:17-19). God had judged that, for this cowardice of striking the feeble, faint, and weary without regard of God, that Amalek would end up with all his lineage being destroy from under heaven. When you decide to not fear the Living God, do not think he does not remember your rebellion, judgement will come on that day that you do not expect.

Saul takes the Israelites to destroy the Amalekites and defeats them; however, instead of utterly destroying everything, Saul saved the King Agag alive and allowed the people to keep the best of the sheep and oxen. God's purpose was to root out all that was tied to the rebellion of Amalek, but Saul allowed the root of the rebellion to remain in the presence of God's people. Samuel confronts Saul with what they have done, and Saul answers with another excuse (1 Samuel 15:13-15). Not only does he give an excuse, but he deceives himself by telling Samuel in verse 13, "I have performed the commandment of the Lord." What Saul is unaware of is God had already spoken with Samuel concerning this rebellion of Saul. By letting the people keep the best of the sheep and oxen to sacrifice unto the Lord, Saul has fallen prey to self-righteous religion. Doing what they think is right but being masked under selfish ambition. Simply put this is rebellion.

Samuel has a very hard truth for this selfish ambition in chapter 15:22-23. No matter what religious rules you may be following to make yourself feel good before God, none is more acceptable to God than simple obedience to his voice. While you may be thinking you're doing a pious act that looks good to those around you, has it really been to justify your actions? Are you obeying his voice? Are you hearing his voice? If you are not hearing the Lord through the Word, or by the Holy Spirit, or God just outright calls on you then you, then you best be finding out why. Start with repentance and go back to what you need to obey him on. In chapter 12, Samuel qualifies himself in his relationship before Israel and God, then goes on to qualify the history of Israel being led out of Egypt by God's hand, which brings him to the current moment they are in. Israel had God for their king but rejected him and settled for an earthly king. In verses 14 and 15, he gave to them the rules of the game for this kingship they wanted: fear the Lord, serve him, obey his voice, and do not rebel. If they do this, then both them and the king will continue to follow the Lord. If, however, they do not obey the voice of the Lord but instead become rebellious against the voice of the Lord, than the hand of the Lord will be against them. Plain and simple truth and not difficult to understand. This was the instruction straight from the mouth of God spoken by the man of God, Samuel. This is exactly what Saul disobeyed.

Samuel called Saul's disobedience rebellion, witchcraft, stubbornness, iniquity, and idolatry. This leads us to rejecting God. It led Saul to rejecting God, and ultimately, it led God to reject Saul from being king.[37]

---

[37] Rebellion; O.T. Hebrew Marah, Strong's 4784

To be rebellious against, to be disobedient toward someone, to be refractory, to rebel, to resist, to despise, to quarrel, to dispute, to offend. Literally, it means to be (or make) bitter or unpleasant. Provocation is an inherent component of this term. The idea is conveyed in this word rather strongly. Hebrew Greek Key Study Bible NASB version with Strong's Dictionary

Rebellion are the conscious decisions we make to become desensitized toward the working of the Holy Spirit. Making yourself dense toward being able to absorb the word of God into your heart. This is why the word refractory is used as a description of the word rebellion. Refractory as we know it today is used in the steel industry or in lining boilers. It is a mixture of minerals that vary in size from powder form to the size of small stone. The idea is when blended together and hardened there are no voids leaving no opening for the molten steel or fire to penetrate. Being an extremely dense lining, it insulates the container from the damaging effects of the heat. In other words, rebellion prevents the fire of God from purifying our hearts, which is a work of the

Saul has been found by God to be defiant, stubborn, and unrepentant. But, you say, in1 Samuel 15:24, Saul says to Samuel, "I have sinned: for I have transgressed the commandment of the Lord" and he even admits how this wrongdoing got started, "I feared the people …" There have been many circumstances in the Bible where people have feared what they were facing, the outcome is always dependent upon their response toward God. All who obeyed God were able to accomplish his word. All who disobeyed God lost much. Saul didn't obey God. Instead, he obeyed the voice of the people (15:24). Now Saul asks for Samuel to pardon his sin so he may worship the Lord. Saul reached rock bottom in his relationship with God here. He had been anointed, stood up under the power of the Holy Spirit, and even prophesized, but when it came time to repent, he turned to Samuel to pardon his sin instead of turning to the One who gave him the commandments, the Lord himself (1 Samuel 15:25-26).

Samuel would have no part in it stating Saul had rejected the word of the Lord in vs. 26. At this point, Saul was faced with the weight of what was occurring, and as Samuel turned to leave, Saul reacted in desperation by reaching out and laying hold of the mantel of Samuel. This action tore the mantel, thereby, signifying that the Lord has torn the kingdom from Saul (1 Samuel 15:27-28).

These are the events that were occurring in Israel the same time a young shepherd boy was protecting the livelihood of his family from wild beasts. These were tumultuous times in Israel, changing times in Israel, and you can bet that the news of these events reached around the country and even to a field with sheep grazing in it. All of Israel heard of, knew of, and feared Samuel because God spoke with him. The elders of the tribes and cities had asked for a king, and you may certainly know that the family of Jesse from Bethlehem discussed it at the dinner table. When Samuel shows up in Bethlehem to anoint the one God has

---

Holy Ghost. It builds a wall around our hearts and stands against the Word of God and the work of the Holy Spirit. Rebellion is a matter of our will.

158

chosen to replace King Saul, the elders were trembling, and now we know why. They feared Samuel because God spoke directly to him. They may well have been included with the elders involved in forcing Samuel to choose an earthly king for them. It is quite possible they were part of those leaders rejecting the Lord as their King and opting for an earthly king (1 Samuel 16:4; 8:4-5). They were also aware of Saul's endeavors and his rejecting God by not obeying his commandments. Samuel, setting them at ease, said he comes peaceably and wants to sacrifice unto the Lord. Samuel has Jesse and his sons come to the sacrifice along with the elders. The elders are there, Jesse and his sons are there, and Samuel is looking around at everyone wondering which one the Lord has chosen to become the next king. He sees the eldest son of Jesse who must have been a tall strapping young man that surely looked the part. He is thinking, *That's got to be the guy* until God sets him straight, "The Lord sees not as man sees, man looks on the outward appearance, but the Lord looks on the heart." (1 Samuel 16:7).

Samuel instructs Jesse to have his sons come and pass before him. This way, he can point out to everyone present who God has chosen to be king. All of Jesse's sons pass by Samuel, and God chose none of them. Samuel is a little perplexed by this and asks, "Are these all the children you have?" If you're a parent, and someone of great importance shows up specifically asking for you and your sons to see, which one is chosen, don't you think you would be fairly curious as to what is going on? Jesse tells Samuel, "I have one more son, the youngest. He is out watching the sheep." Samuel says go get him because we are not sitting down until he shows up.[38]

---

[38] David was charged with watching the sheep while the rest of the family got to be with the important people of the community. What was the reason for this? Why wasn't he included with the rest of the family? Oftentimes, families, because they are so closely involved with each other, will develop preconceived ideas towards each other. We have already seen that God looks on the heart of a man. He knows what's cooking in your head and inner most being. We see the outside, the incidents that occur that cause us to make judgements that are often unwarranted. If there was someone available to watch the sheep when they went to get David that person was more than likely available earlier so David could have been included from the start. We see a touch of this preconceived thinking when Jesse sends David with bread

David has now embarked on a journey that will cover many years, involve many conflicts, and require wise counsel and the need for great dependence on God. He will bring together everyone that is in distress, in debt, and discontented with what life was throwing at them during this time in Israel (1 Samuel 22:2). He would endure threats on his life, people who would betray him out of loyalty to Saul, living in caves, seeing those who gave him a helping hand be killed by Saul, and still, he relied on the Holy Spirit's guidance and comfort. From his world renowned defeat of the giant Goliath to the death of the priest Ahimelech at the city of Nob by the hand of Saul (1 Samuel chapters 17; 21; and 22), to the many battles David fought, to the troubles he encountered amongst his own children as he got older, David always turned to the Lord.

Stark Differences

When we look at these two men, Saul and David, we see some stark differences between the two. Both were anointed to be king, and both had the Holy Spirit come upon them, but each one treated the anointing differently. Each man received the Holy Spirit, but only one man relied on and listened to the Spirit (1 Samuel 16:14; 18:12;) while the other never mentioned or recognized the work of the Holy Spirit.

---

and cheese to the battle front to check on his brothers. In 1 Samuel 17:28 David's oldest brother, Eliab, gets angry with David when he is questioning the soldiers about Goliath and why he is defying the armies of the Lord. Read the story, and you will see that Goliath had been belching out his defiance for forty days, and Eliab was amongst the army of Israel that feared this giant of a man all this time. When David shows up for such a brief time, and his first response is, "… who is this uncircumcised Philistine, that he should defy the armies of the living God?" (1 Samuel 17:26), it is easy to see the frustration that boils up out of Eliab's heart. He had been passed over by Samuel and not anointed by God because God knew his heart. If you are called by God to his work, never let your family"s preconceived ideas about you distract your heart from trusting and knowing God. This is why God chose David to be anointed in the midst of his brothers. This is why later on the entire family joined David and his band of distressed and broken people. This is a representation of Jesus who comes to heal the broken hearted and bring unity.

Saul, however, was keenly aware that God had removed the Holy Spirit from him (1 Samuel 16:14; 18:12; 28:5-6 and15). Let's delve into each man and see what caused them to be different amid some of the same circumstances.

First and foremost, we look at the title of this chapter, "Give Thanks." Nowhere do we see Saul ever giving thanks to God for anything. David, however, is found many times to have given thanks to God. In 1 Chronicles 16, David even set up people whose responsibilities were to give thanks and praise to God. 1 Chronicles 16:4 reads, "And he appointed certain of the Levites to minister before the ark of the Lord, and to record, and to thank and praise the Lord God of Israel. Verse 7 and 8 read, "Then on that day David delivered first this psalm to thank the Lord into the hand of Asaph and his brethren. Give thanks unto the Lord, call upon his name, make known his deeds among the people." Verse 29 reads, "Give unto the Lord the glory due unto his name: bring an offering, and come before him: worship the Lord in the beauty of holiness." Verse 34 and 35 read, "O give thanks unto the Lord: for he is good; for his mercy endures forever. And say ye, Save us O God of our salvation, and gather the heathen, that we may give thanks to thy holy name, and glory in thy praise." Verse 41reads, "And with them Heman and Jeduthun, and the rest that were chosen, who were expressed by name, to give thanks to the Lord, because his mercy endures forever."

Saul rejected the commands of the Lord given to him in his endeavors as king (1 Samuel 13:13; 15:11 and 19).

David did as God commanded, and it caused him to be successful, which brought a fear of him to all nations (1 Chronicles 14:16 and 17).

Saul lived in fear, showing concern for what was facing him, whether it be the Philistines, or the people of Israel themselves. He had not faith and trust in his heart (1 Samuel 13:11-12; 15:24; 28:5; 18:12).

Saul had jealousy in his heart. This is what he thought about. He looked at others perceiving them to be a threat (1 Samuel 18:6-9). It drove him to bitterness and deeper into fear.

David inquired of the Lord countless times finding encouragement, direction, and instruction (1 Samuel 23:2-4; 30:6-8; 2 Samuel 2:1; 1 Chronicles 14:10,14-15).

David understood the anointing was from the Lord God, and you don't mess with the anointing, nor grieve the Holy Spirit. Having the anointing and the Holy Spirit of the Living God meant a great deal to him (1 Samuel 26:9; 24:6; I Chronicles 16:22; Psalm 51:10-12; Psalm 20:6). Giving respect to the Holy Spirit is what David followed many times during his life and reign as king. This respect came from his love for the Holy Spirit and for the love the Holy Spirit put in David's heart.

Whatever time David was faced with, an event that caused him to fear, or distress, he turned to the Lord (1 Samuel 30:6-8; Psalm 56:3,4).

Saul decided to glorify himself instead of obeying the command of the Lord. In 1 Samuel 15:12, Saul had gone to Carmel after fighting with the Amalekites and set up a monument to himself. Not only had he rejected the Word of God by not doing what he was commanded to do, but now he made it about himself. This is typically the path we follow when we lie to ourselves, thinking we have done the will of God, when, instead, we fell short. Where do you go from this point? God gives us our breath for life. He gives us the rain and the sun. He gives us wisdom and knowledge and understanding. But he will not give his glory to anyone, period (Isaiah 42:8; 48:11)! This is his part. This is his greatness. This is us as created. This is not for us. When you fail to accomplish his Word and take it as though it is by you that it is accomplished, you have deceived yourself. Do not think yourself to be something you're not. Above all, do not try to take his glory. You will be brought to the end of yourself. But God has no end. He is forever and ever.

Remember, he is not willing that any should parish but that all come to repentance (2 Peter 3:9). But if we reject his Word, his voice, his commands, and his opportunity, than He will most certainly reject us. As He did with Saul, so shall he do with those who choose not to believe and those who do not repent from their rebellious attitudes, thoughts, and self-justifications that draw glory to themselves. His judgement will come quickly (2 Peter 3:10).

David repeatedly gave the praise to God for his deliverance by giving thanks. By speaking out, confessing out loud that it was God who strengthened him, saved him, protected him. Read the Psalms and relate them with the events that as they happened to David, and you will see them in a different light possibly. Psalm 51 is what David confessed after Nathan the prophet exposed David's sin when he went into Bath-sheba (2 Samuel 11). In Psalm 18, David poured out his heart to the Lord in the day the Lord delivered him out of the hand of Saul and the hand of all his enemies (2 Samuel 5:12; 7:24-29). Psalm 56 where David had first fled from Saul to Gath, the land of the Philistines, Goliath's homeland, and had to act like a mad man so the Philistines would not come against him (1 Samuel 22). Through all this ordeal, what does he have to say but that he has put his trust in God, and he would not fear what man can do to him (Psalm 56:11). The Lord is nigh unto all that call upon the Lord in truth (Psalm 145:18-20).

David's life is a declaration of life itself that all of us face even today. The battles for integrity, for how we perceive our Father in heaven, for the thoughts we think toward him and others, all of this is before him. When we call upon him in truth (his Word is truth) then he is near. How is that? Because when you live in his Word, his truth, and you call upon him as David did, then you are in life because he is life (John 5:26; 6:51; 14:6).

As you read of the life of David in 1 and 2 Samuel, 1 Kings, and 1 Chronicles, you will see a life that faced challenges that were hard and difficult, you will see deep emotions and hurts, but you will also see tremendous victories amidst the fulfilling of God's Word through David's obedience, faith, trust, and reliance each time he fell and each time he repented. Through the entire campaign of his life, he gave thanks to God by acknowledging his sovereignty as the Creator, Deliverer and Savior. Giving thanks to God will always produce praise, which is the greatest way to give thanks to God. The book of Psalms ends with the last three chapters - 148,149, and 150 - where David is giving praise to God for everything that lives and moves on this earth. David gives us the secret that others in the Bible and in the world today share that propels them into his presence when he spoke in Psalm 57:7-11, "My heart is fixed (steadfast), O God my heart is fixed: I will sing and give praise." A settled heart is a heart that is at rest and peace, confident in strength and courage, knowing, wise, and understanding.

Just as Daniel settled in his heart to obey God and follow his commandments, so, too, David fixed his heart to follow God's commands. It takes grit and humility to determine that you will give God your life without regard for yourself. It doesn't just happen. You must overcome distractions and capture those thoughts that are contrary to life in Christ. It is doable. We are able to attain to a heart such as this. We must know it is a lifetime of yielding to him, confessing when we slip, trusting him for our deliverance and salvation. Do it by giving thanks and entering his courts with praise because this is what David did. He did not live a perfect life, but he lived life perfectly trusting his Father in heaven.

Apostle John

Let us move on to our third example in the Apostle John. There is much that may be studied and read about the Apostle John from historical writings by many authors through the centuries. Some you may find factual, some heretical, some misleading and some sprinkled with truth and fiction. But this is not why we are here. We are not here to dispute what others have written, how it may have happened, or didn't happen in history. Rather, we are here to delve into his relationship with the Savior and what this means to us today.

We find in the Gospels two families that formed a partnership in the fishing business with each family having sons involved in the business. One son had been following a prophet of a man named John the Baptist. A day came when Jesus approached John the Baptist to be baptized. John the Baptist had been preaching to the people to repent and that someone was coming who was greater than himself. This one son named Andrew happened to be the brother of the man who would become known as Peter. Andrew sees Jesus being baptized and witnesses the Holy Spirit of God descend from heaven upon Jesus. This is quit an extraordinary event. Andrew goes back home and tells his brother of these events. The other partners of Andrew and Peter and their father, Jona, were James, John, and their father, Zebedee. These two families were working together and very likely had conversations discussing John the Baptist and this man, Jesus, and about the Holy Spirit coming down upon Jesus like a dove, and about the voice coming from heaven declaring, "This is my beloved Son, in whom I am well pleased." (Matthew 3:17).. Andrew was convinced the Messiah spoken of by Moses and the prophets was most certainly this man, Jesus.

The fishing business usually was done during the night so by morning, they would have product to sell to the people during the day. Now Jesus comes along and sees these two ships with the families and hired servants cleaning up from the previous night of fishing. It just so happens it wasn't a good night for fishing because they had caught nothing. Jesus tells Simon Peter to launch out into the deep and let down his nets for a catch. We know that Andrew had already told his brother Peter about Jesus, so Peter decided to follow the command of this man. Peter explains that they had toiled all night and caught nothing (Luke 5:5). We also know that before this happened that Peter's Mother-in-law had a great fever of which Jesus rebuked and she was made well (Luke 4:38,39). It makes sense that an experienced fisherman who did this for a living would even think about listening to a man telling him how to fish if he hadn't had a good reason to listen. He saw his Mother-in-law healed and listened to his brother telling him this guy is who all of Israel had been waiting for all these centuries. "Nevertheless, at thy word I will let down the net." Peter spoke (Luke 5:5).

Well, the story goes that there were so many fish that the net began to break, and they called their partner with the other ship to come to help. As we go on to read the account of Jesus picking his disciples, we see he comes to James and John mending their nets. They were mending their nets because they just experienced this miracle of the great catch of fish that tore their nets. When Jesus says come and follow me, they forsook their nets and followed him (Mark 1:17-18). Andrew, Peter, James, and John were now following Jesus. This was John's introduction to becoming a disciple and later on an apostle. John, being a young man, witnessing these events certainly did leave quit an impression on him.

John has officially joined the ministry of Jesus. He listens to Jesus preach and teach these next three years. He watches people being healed of all manner of sickness. He sees the dead raised back to life. He observes and listens to the criticisms of the Scribes and Pharisee religious leaders. He is involved in baptizing people as they repent and believe. He witnessed countless miracles, the feeding of thousands from a small portion, the calming of the wind, storm, and waves while at sea on a ship, even being startled at Jesus walking upon the water and much, much more. He had to be learning about himself, about the law and the prophets and how it pointed to this time in history, about giving to others, about taking what Jesus spoke as truth and applying it to life, and about knowing Jesus is the Son of God, the Messiah. These are the events that began to mold a young man into a true disciple of Jesus.

Being a fisherman for a livelihood is not an easy business. It is hard labor coupled with knowing the mechanics of shipping and maintaining equipment. Developing a practical approach to things is a requirement, so to speak. John has this practical straight forward approach to life that is now being infused with knowledge of the Word of God, the miracles of Jesus, and the faith of the Father. We see this practical approach in John 12:4-6 as Mary anointed the feet of Jesus. Earlier in this book we touched on this story but it bears repeating do to the significance of the structure of this story. John explains that Judas Iscariot questioned the use of such expensive ointment as to why it wasn't sold so they could give to the poor. This story is accounted for in the other Gospels, but John doesn't mince words, or mask how he felt about Judas here. He flat out called him a thief! Judas was skimming money out of the purse for himself. What Mary did to Jesus was for his honor. What Judas did was for his own self-satisfaction. The obvious tone John takes here towards the man that would betray Jesus is the straightforward acknowledgement that what Judas Iscariot had done was an evil act towards the Messiah. He called it what it was. Mary's heart was full of love for the one who forgave her of her sins. Judas' heart was full of greed for money. No wonder the word of God tells us money is the root of all evil. The main point here is that in all aspects of our lives, there is a choice to make, this example John wrote of demonstrates the difference of where our choices lead us to, and what we give to those choices, and what we take from those choices.

During another time, John, his brother James, and Peter went with Jesus up into a mountain to pray. While Jesus was praying, Peter, James and John were heavy with sleep, but when they woke up, they saw an amazing sight. There was Jesus, transfigured in body and clothing, standing talking with Moses and Elijah in glory. Two of the greatest men in Israel's history standing before them in glory, talking with the man they were following. What a moment to experience.

It is apparent that these events along with his practical approach to things coupled with hanging around that fiery fellow Peter had John's enthusiasm running pretty high. Jesus early on named James and John, "The Sons of Thunder" (Mark 3:17). In Luke 9:51-56, Jesus had set himself to go to Jerusalem because his time was coming to an end. On the way, they stopped in a small town in Samaria, but the people there did not receive them because it was obvious the focus of Jesus and the disciples was on going to Jerusalem. James and John took this as an offense towards Jesus. They asked Jesus if he wanted them to call down fire from heaven to consume them. What they got from Jesus was a stern rebuke, "You do not know what manner of spirit you are of." Enthusiasm, excitement, intensity, and inexperience may accomplish some things for you in this world, but they certainly fall short of working and moving in the Holy Ghost. Jesus was not here to destroy them but to fulfill what the Father said and to save them. No matter where you are in your relationship with Christ, do not turn away a rebuke done in truth and love. You may not like it but that is just your-self sin nature whining. When you get into the Spirit, you accept it and grow. Better to be rebuked by the Lord than to be rejected by Him.

There is much more we could learn about John during the time in ministry with Jesus, but it is time to look at how he is growing in his relationship with the master. Look at John chapters 13 through 17, and you will see Jesus talking with the Father while teaching his disciples showing what has been given him and what has been given to us. Jesus points everything to the Father and fulfilling his will. In these chapters, we see the relationship John had with the Christ. Read them thoroughly over and over again. You will see John reveal to us the heart of Jesus that he is here to do the will of his Father, he is here to go and prepare a place for us, he is here to instruct us on how to believe, he is here to raise a banner for the world to see and that banner is we are to love one another. We are to love him.

In Matthew 22:37-40, Jesus speaks of the two great commandments. A commandment is an order to be carried out at all costs. If a commandment is not followed, then a judgement will be rendered on the disobedience. The first commandment is, "You shall love the Lord your God with all your heart, with all your soul and with all your mind." (thoughts). The second commandment is like the first you shall, "love

168

your neighbor as yourself." These two commandments are what all the law and all the prophets depended on, lived on, died on, and spoke on.

When you have it settled in your mind and heart to love the Lord your God, when you no longer argue with yourself about obedience to his word, when you no longer entertain thoughts to justify yourself, than you will find it easy to love your neighbor as yourself. How? Why? Because the love you are giving out is not your own. It is the Lord's. His love dwells in you and you dwell in his love (I John 4:16). John expresses to us in 1 John that God is love; how that Jesus shed his own blood by the grueling painful death of crucifixion so that we may have our sin cleansed and redeemed from the curse. We come to know him by keeping his commandments and by doing so we are doing the will of God. We know we have the Holy Ghost to teach us. We know that God loved us because he sent his Son for us. We know that by keeping his commandments, we get his love.

Long about now, you are probably asking, "Where is the giving thanks by John?" Well, it isn't in there. Why would the Lord have me write about an example of giving thanks if it doesn't show up in the scriptures? Because this is a deeper life. John came to understand that he is loved by God himself, by Jesus, and by the Holy Spirit. His love for God was matured to the point he had no fear. It was cast out of him by the indwelling of God's love. When you are enveloped by this much love, the giving of thanks simply comes pouring out of this source of love in your heart, because there is no self in you to fight against it. It becomes like breathing at this point. I know everyone out there needs love, wants to be loved, and hopes for love no matter how far down this world has pushed them. We may look in all the different ways the world offers, but we will never find it the way God gives it unless we look to him for it.

It is like John describes in Revelation 4:8-9 where he is telling us about four creatures who cry out in verse 8, "Holy, holy, holy, Lord God Almighty, which was, and is, and is to come." In verse 9 every time "they give glory and honor and thanks to him that sat on the throne, who lives for ever and ever.," the twenty four elders fall down and worship. These creatures do not rest day and night giving glory and honor and thanks to God. It pours out of them. This is how it was with John by knowing and living in his love, a thankful heart just pours out of him. You cannot give out love and not have a thankful heart. They work together. As you give thanks to God, he gives love to you.

Let's take one more look at a moment for John that transcends history itself. This is so impactful and so full of emotion that we are afraid to get close to it ourselves. Each of the four Gospels give that writers personal experience of the crucifixion. John, however, takes it to a perspective that is deeply personal demonstrating a closeness in his relationship with Jesus.

Matthew, Mark, and Luke each include a group of women who stood afar off watching the crucifixion unfold before them (Matthew 27:55; Mark 15:40; Luke 23:49). John gives us a detail the others left out. Exactly where Matthew, Mark and Luke were at during the crucifixion the Scriptures do not indicate. John's rendition tells us a different viewpoint of who was there and where they were. John 19:25 reads, "Now there stood by the cross ..." they weren't afar off. They were by the cross. Besides the women, John was standing there also. John's rendition gives an up close and personal view of what was going on. First, he gives a more complete view of the women who were there, and he also includes the disciple who Jesus loved. He doesn't give his name. He gives us his relationship status: This isn't about him. It is about Jesus, and John's writings reflect this.

Now this suffering they were all witnessing takes an even deeper emotional draw. Jesus, from up on the cross, bleeding, in great anguish and pain, having difficulties breathing due to the weight of his body bearing down, looks down and sees John standing next to his Mother Mary and says, "Woman, behold thy son!" and follows that with words to John, "Behold thy Mother." (John 19:26-27). Jesus would not trust the welfare of his mother to someone he did not love. John knew Jesus loved him, and he received the honor of taking care of Jesus' mother.

As you look at the crucifixion, there is much to learn, but I want to point out two things that stand out. One being all the people that railed against Christ, mocking him, spitting on him, and shaking their heads in disgust, all did so from a position of hate. They did not hate Jesus for his miracles nor for the authority he taught with. They hated him because they were forced with a choice to choose to follow him, or hang onto their self-justifications, their positions held amongst men, and their fear of letting go of what they had and giving it back to God. Mocking is simply a form of hiding your own faults. Hate wants only vindication but does not like to watch the suffering.

The second point is about those who stood at the foot of the cross and watched the suffering in the pain of love. Love stays through the suffering! This is where we find the Apostle John standing at the foot of the cross, in humility, in honor and deep love. This is what transcended history. This is what led this man to write about the heart of Jesus. This is what leads us to the love of God. Do we actually find the words of John saying thanks to God in the scriptures? Maybe not, but we see this giving of thanks being poured out by the expressions of love he demonstrates in his writings. You cannot love this deeply and not have a thankful heart. You see it in the Gospel of John, you see it in the epistles 1, 2, and 3 John and in the book of the Revelation of Jesus the Christ. We may not grasp this yet, but it is there for us. He is always there for us at any time we turn to Him. John gave thanks to God by the life he lived and the words he wrote for us to learn about Jesus.

Wrap Up

We have looked at Daniel, David, and the Apostle John how each gave thanks to God by having a settled mind. They weren't tossed about by every wind of doctrine. They looked to their Creator and thanked him for forgiving their sins, their family's sins, and the sins of the nation.

John knew what repentance was since he heard both John the Baptist and Jesus preach repentance. All three of these men loved God, and he loved them back. Look at the relationship they had with God. Daniel had an excellent spirit. David was a man after God's own heart, and John was the disciple whom Jesus loved. This stuff doesn't just happen it is built through trials, decisions we make, repentance when we fall, trust that stands against doubt and insecurities, and a love that grows each time it is tested.

If you are one of us who never gave a lot of thought to giving thanks, or maybe you did it out of habit, don't you think it is time to start applying God's word and what he commands us. In everything give thanks for this *is the will of God*. As you give thanks for his sovereignty, you will find his love will be readily available to you. You will find the situations you encounter in this life will begin to take on a different atmosphere.

Praise God, surrender yourself, and give Him thanks continually, gratefully, graciously, and in truth from the heart for his love.

"You live, not to receive from the Father,

But to give to the Father."

-Shellie Read.

GOOD WORD

The following comprises quotations I have written in my Bible over the years from those I have sat under and heard the Word of God preached. It also includes the words I have received from the Holy Spirit and the Father as they revealed them to me at different times in my life. I have given you as well a list of verses that contain some of the give and the take contained in the Word of God.

"Humility is my utter acceptance of my continual dependence on Yaweh."

(David Read)

"The love of God will draw people to repentance."

(Diane Sumrall)

"He is as forgiving as He is Holy. He is as patient as He is perfect."

(David Read)

"There is no value that can be put on a soul. God can afford it. He has redeemed that value already. You be willing to do as He says."

(Ephriam Mutabo)

"And I will *give* this people favour in the sight of the Egyptians: and it shall come to pass that, when ye go, ye shall not go empty:"
(Exodus 3:21)

"And said, Naked came I out of my mother's womb, and naked shall I return thither: the Lord *gave*, and the Lord hath *taken* away; blessed be the name of the Lord." (Job 1:21)

"For in death there is no remembrance of thee: in the grave who shall *give* thee thanks." (Psalm 6:5)

"For thou desirest not sacrifice; else would I *give* it: thou delightest not in burnt offering. The sacrifices of God are a broken spirit: a broken and a contrite heart; O God, thou wilt not despise." (Psalm 51:16-17)

"Therefore the Lord himself shall *give* you a sign; Behold, a virgin shall conceive, and bear a son, and shall call his name Immanuel." (Isaiah 7:14)

"Incline your ear, and come unto me: hear, and your soul shall live; and I will make an everlasting covenant with you, even the sure mercies of David. Behold I have *given* him for a witness to the people, a leader and commander to the people." (Isaiah 55:3-4)

"Great in counsel, and mighty in work: for thine eyes are open upon all the ways of the sons of men: to *give* every one according to his ways, and according to the fruit of his doings." (Jeremiah 32:19)

"For I will *take* you from among the heathen, and gather you out of all countries, and will bring you into your own land." (Ezekiel 36:24)

"Then was the king exceeding glad for him, and commanded that they should *take* Daniel up out of the den. So Daniel was *taken* up out of the den, and no manner of hurt was found upon him, because he believed in his God." Daniel 6:23

"Be glad then, ye children of Zion, and rejoice in the Lord your God: for he hath *given* you the former rain moderately and he will cause to come down for you the rain, the former rain, and the latter rain in the first month." (Joel 2:23)

"But I will sacrifice unto thee with the voice of *thanksgiving*; I will pay that that I have vowed. Salvation is of the Lord." (Jonah 2:9)

"In that day shalt thou not be ashamed for all thy doings, wherein thou has transgressed against me: for then I will *take* away out of the midst of thee them that rejoice in thy pride, and thou shalt no more be haughty because of my holy mountain." (Zephaniah 3:11)

"My covenant was with him of life and peace: and I *gave* them to him for the fear wherewith he feared me, and was afraid before my name." (Malachi 2:5)

"Therefore I say unto you, *Take* no thought for your life, what ye shall eat, or what ye shall drink; nor yet for your body, what ye shall put on. Is not the life more than meat, and the body than raiment?" (Matthew 6:25)

"Ask and it shall be *given* you; seek, and ye shall find; knock and it shall be opened unto you:" (Matthew 7:7)

"Come unto me, all ye that labour and are heavy laden, and I will *give* you rest. *Take* my yoke upon you, and learn of me: for I am meek and lowly in heart and ye shall find rest unto your souls." (Matthew11:28-29)

"And when he had called the people unto him with his disciples also, he said unto them, Whosoever will come after me, let him deny himself, and *take* up his cross, and follow me." "Or what shall a man *give* in exchange for his soul?" (Mark 8:34 and 37)

"And as they did eat, Jesus took bread, and blessed, and brake it, and *gave* to them, and said, *Take*, eat: this is my body. And he *took* the cup, and when he had *given* thanks, he *gave* it to them: and they all drank of it." (Mark 14:22-23)

"Give, and it shall be given unto you; good measure, pressed down, and shaken together, and running over, shall men give into your bosom…" (Luke 6:38)

"If ye then, being evil, know how to *give* good gifts unto your children: how much more shall your heavenly Father *give* the Holy Spirit to them that ask him?" (Luke 11:13)

"For as the Father hath life in himself: so hath he *given* to the Son to have life in himself; And hath *given* him authority to execute judgment also, because he is the Son of man." (John 5:26-27)

"For the bread of God is he which cometh down from heaven, and *giveth* life unto the world." (John 6:33)

"For I have not spoken of myself; but the Father which sent me, he *gave* me a commandment, what I should say, and what I should speak. And I know that his commandment is life everlasting: whatsoever I speak therefore, even as the Father said unto me, so I speak." (John 12:50)

"And I will pray the Father, and he shall *give* you another Comforter, that he may abide with you forever." (John14:16)

"But we will *give* ourselves continually to prayer, and to the ministry of the word." (Acts 6:4)

"And even as they did not like to retain God in their knowledge, God *gave* them over to a reprobate mind, to do those things which are not convenient;" (Romans 1:28)

"There hath no temptation *taken* you but such as is common to man: but God is faithful, who will not suffer you to be tempted above that ye are able;" (1 Corinthians 10:13)

"But the manifestation of the Spirit is *given* to every man to profit withal." (1 Corinthians 12:7)

"But thanks be to God, which *giveth* us the victory through our Lord Jesus Christ." (1 Corinthians 15:57)

"Every man according as he purposeth in his heart, so let him *give*; not grudgingly, or of necessity: for God loveth a cheerful *giver*." (2 Corinthians 9:7)

"And walk in love, as Christ also hath loved us, and hath *given* himself for us an offering and a sacrifice to God for a sweetsmelling savour." (Ephesians 5:2)

"Husbands, love your wives, even as Christ also loved the church, and *gave* himself for it;" (Ephesians 5:25)

"Above all, *taking* the shield of faith, wherewith ye shall be able to quench all the fiery darts of the wicked. And *take* the helmet of salvation, and the sword of the Spirit, which is the word of God." (Ephesians 6:16)

"Wherefore God also hath highly exalted him, and *given* him a name which is above every name:" (Philippians 2:9)

"And whatsoever ye do in word or deed, do all in the name of the Lord Jesus, *giving* thanks to God and the Father by him." (Colossians 3:17)

"But he *giveth* more grace. Wherefore he saith, God resisteth the proud, but *giveth* grace unto the humble." (James 4:6)

"The bigger the personal vision you have the bigger the personal battles you will face. You cannot have big victories without big battles." (Lester Sumrall)

"The greatest miracle is when Jesus forgives you and you are saved. All other miracles are lesser. If you have faith for the greater you can believe for the lesser."(R.W. Schambach)

"When you stay in His presence you develop the ability to lose the cares of this world." (Gary Cooper on Psalm 16:11)

"Then said he, Lo, I come to do thy will, O God. He *taketh* away the first, that he may establish the second. By the which will we are sanctified through the offering of the body of Jesus Christ once for all. And every priest standeth daily ministering and offering oftentimes the same sacrifices, which can never *take* away sins: But this man, after he had offered one sacrifice for sins forever, sat down on the right hand of God;" (Hebrews 10:9-12)

"And the glory which thou *gavest* me I have *given* them; that they may be one, even as we are one:" (John 17:22)

"And ye shall serve the Lord your God, and he shall bless thy bread, and thy water; and I will *take* away sickness away from the midst of thee." (Exodus 23:25)

Give-and-take is an action. It requires you to do something. It becomes an act of your will. Give in love, from love and out of love. Take the promise of the Word in truth and live.

"...for the Lord your God proveth you, to know whether ye love the Lord your God with all your heart and with all your soul." (Deuteronomy 13:3)

Be a Servant to the Father and your Neighbor, for a servant gives to the Master and takes commands from the Master.

REFERENCES

https://biblehub.com, copyright (2004-2019) by Bible Hub.

New American Standard Bible Copyright 1960, 1962, 1968, 1971, 1972, 1973, 1975, 1977, The Lockman Foundation. A Corporation Not for Profit, La Habra, Califronia

Simpson, A. B. (1984). Days of Heaven on Earth. Christian Publications Camp Hill, PA

Publishing House of the Christian and Missionary Alliance.

3825 Hartzdale Drive, Camp Hill PA 17011

 Library of Congress Catalog Card No. 84-70150.

Printed in the United States of America.

The Holy Bible Old and New Testaments in the King James Version (1972). Kenneth Copland Edition with a reader's guide to exploring the Bible. Copyright 1972 by Thomas Nelson Inc. Nashville/ Camden/New York

Printed in the United States of America.

Zodhiates, Spiros Th. D. Compiled and edited (Copyright 1984, 1990). The Hebrew Greek Key Study Bible New American Standard with Strong's Dictionary, Word Studies and Concordance. Zodhiates' original and complete system of Bible study. AMG Publishers. Chattanooga, TN 37422 U.S.A.

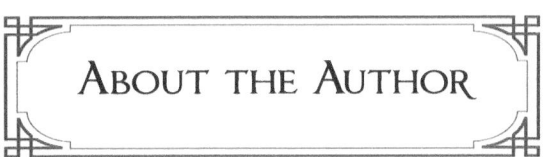

ABOUT THE AUTHOR

In 2016 God spoke to David telling him to write a book and to title it Give and Take. God in his persistence convinced David to get started and this is the book. Along the way as God revealed to him what to write he was confronted with addressing the short-comings in his spiritual life and went through a maturing process in his own spirit and soul.

David A. Read grew up in a rural small town in Northern Indiana dividing his time between coaching Jr. high school teams, running his co-owned business as well as working for large corporations. After getting married and having three children with his best friend and wife God began qualifying him and pressing him to stop living for himself and begin to know the Lord more.

As Paul the Apostle wrote in Philippians 3:7-13 about all that he had gained he counted as loss being measured against knowing Jesus the Christ and yet realizing he had not yet obtained to this knowledge he continued to press forward toward that mark of knowing Christ and the power of his resurrection. So too, David, continues toward that mark amidst all the happenings and events of the world today always pressing forward amongst the trials and victories coming to know he is loved by God, by Jesus, and the indwelling of the Holy Spirit.